INDIAN MASTERS OF ENGLISH

INDIAN MASTERS OF ENGLISH

AN ANTHOLOGY OF ENGLISH PROSE BY INDIAN WRITERS

BY

E. E. SPEIGHT, B.A.

GYAN

Published by

Gyan Publishing House
5, Ansari Road
Daryaganj, New Delhi-110002
Phone: 011-47034999, 9811692060
E-mail: books@gyanbooks.com

Distribution Network
gyanbooks.com
India, USA, Canada, UK, Australia

ISBN: 978-93-6208-351-7 (PB)
First Published, 1934

2nd Impression 2024

Printed at: Gyan Press, Delhi.

INDIAN MASTERS OF ENGLISH
Author: E. E SPEIGHT

INDIAN MASTERS OF ENGLISH

INDIAN MASTERS OF ENGLISH

AN ANTHOLOGY OF ENGLISH PROSE BY INDIAN WRITERS

SELECTED AND EDITED

BY

E. E. SPEIGHT, B.A.

SENIOR PROFESSOR OF ENGLISH IN THE OSMANIA UNIVERSITY
HYDERABAD

FORMERLY OF THE IMPERIAL UNIVERSITY, TOKYO

Author of

A *High School Composition* for Indian Schools

LONGMANS, GREEN AND CO. LTD.
6 OLD COURT HOUSE STREET, CALCUTTA
53 NICOL ROAD, BOMBAY
36A MOUNT ROAD, MADRAS
LONDON, NEW YORK AND TORONTO
1934

DEDICATED

IN AFFECTIONATE GRATITUDE

TO THE MEMORY OF

SIR GEORGE BIRDWOOD

UNDER WHOSE UNSPARING AND SYMPATHETIC GUIDANCE

I FIRST BECAME AWARE OF

INDIA

AS A TREASURE OF THE HUMAN SPIRIT

PREFACE

The preparation of this little book has only been made possible by the very kind help of a number of friends who have enabled me to include some of my many favourite passages from their writings. In the case of Mrs. Naidu, Mr. Abdulla Yusuf Ali, Mr. A. S. Wadia, the Rt. Hon'ble V. S. Srinivasa Sastri and Sir Syed Ross Masood complete freedom of choice was generously granted. Sir Jagadis Chandra Bose has kindly revised his Convocation Address at the University of Mysore in 1927 for inclusion in this book, and Mr. Gandhi, disclaiming, like Mr. Srinivasa Sastri, all insistence on copyright, was so good as to place these three familiar discourses at my disposal. I have to tender my gratitude to all the masters of English represented in this book for their most courteous and welcome collaboration in the making of it.

ACKNOWLEDGMENTS

The thanks of the Editor and the Publishers are due to the following for permission to use the copyright selections included in this book.

Miss Evelyn Gedge for Miss S. Sorabji's 'Srimati Ramabai Ranade' from *Women in Modern India.*

Mr. A. Yusuf Ali and Messrs. Rai Sahib M. Gulab Singh & Sons for 'François Bernier in India' from *Three Travellers to India.*

Dr. Rabindranath Tagore and Messrs. Macmillan & Co. Ltd. for 'The Home-Coming' from *Hungry Stones and other Stories.*

Sir Syed Ross Masood and the Home Secretary to H. E. H. the Nizam's Government for 'Japan' from *Japan and its Educational System.*

Mrs. Sarojini Naidu for 'Gokhale the Man'.

Messrs. G. A. Natesan & Co. for 'Two Addresses' from the *Speeches and Writings of G. K. Gokhale.*

Mr. Dhan Gopal Mukerji and Messrs. E. P. Dutton & Co. for 'The Young Elephant' from *The Chief of the Herd.*

Mr. Salim A. Ali and the Editor of the *Journal of Bombay Natural History Society* for 'The Weaver Bird'.

Mr. A. S. Wadia for the 'English Home' from *The Call of the World.*

The Rt. Hon. V. S. Srinivasa Sastri for 'Rights and Duties' from his *Kamala Lectures.*

The Author's Executors and Messrs. Macmillan & Co. Ltd. for 'The Humanity of Saladin' from *A Short History of the Saracens.*

Mr. M. W. Pickthall, the Editor of *Islamic Culture* for 'Islamic Culture under the Moguls' by Syed Ameer Ali from *Islamic Culture, Oct. 1927.*

Sir J. C. Bose for 'The Greater India To Be'.

Mahatma Gandhi for 'Three Addresses' from his *Broadcast Speeches.*

CONTENTS

INTRODUCTION

THIS little book, which has been in my mind for some years, has been compiled to give Indian students a series of models of what can be done by elder students of their own nationality in the handling of so difficult a language as English. Here they will find striking examples of the command of English in various directions, the character-sketch, historical narrative, the short story, ethical exhortation, nature study, description of social conditions, legal definition and religion. And they will find more than this, for the selections have been chosen not only as testimony to the ability which is placing a number of Indian authors in the very front rank of writers of English, but for the charm of personality, the range of sympathies, which they reveal.

It has been my lot for more than ten years to be shown English prose and verse from every part of India, very varying in quality, and dealing with a very wide range of subjects, from homely scenes and characters to the most intricate matters of economic, aesthetic or philosophical interest, and though I am often asked to devote my little leisure from my constant work with over two hundred students to the revision of pages enough in quantity to daunt a professional proof-reader, the meaning behind all this endeavour never fails to stir me with astonishment. The men and women who have written the following pages stand for me as symbols of a power of adaptation which is so much more astonishing because it comes from people who in other ways are so conservative.

They are representatives of thousands all over India, who already speak more than one Indian language, and yet have taken the trouble to master such a reluctant medium as English. They are like those plants we read of in the dense forests of South America, which have to struggle upwards and upwards to reach their share of the sunlight necessary to the only life that will satisfy them. This energy and determination make a double appeal to me, for I have lived for fifteen years among the ablest young men of the Japanese Empire, helping during that time some thousands of severely selected students, in the most renowned of provincial colleges, and in the Imperial University of Tokyo, through the intricacies of the English language. That was a time for me of wonderful revelations of character, of the flowering of the great Mongol race in that distant chain of volcanic islands where men and nature are engaged in continual warfare often of a terrible nature.

The Japanese, as their amazing progress increasingly shows, are the most astonishingly adaptive people in the world in many ways. Yet not,—with distinguished exceptions, of course,—as linguists. They are as intensely practical by nature as the English, but less gifted than they in that power to become entirely absorbed in the foreign atmosphere which is necessary to the mastery of a foreign language. In that way they form a strong contrast with the educated classes in India, where there are so many languages and dialects and where English has everywhere a unifying function to perform, as well as being the medium of intercourse with the rest of the world. The Japanese cast their feelers everywhere and owe no allegiance to any power but their own. That is at once their strength and their weakness. By that very unwillingness to concentrate on self-expression in any other language than their own they maintain an isolation that is not without danger. India, by freely turning to English and becoming so adept in it, is constantly establishing sympathetic contact of inestimable value with the expanding world employing English speech.

And how admirably well and effectively this is being done! In all this wonderful time of surprising development and discovery there is surely nothing more remarkable than that so many thinkers and writers of India, of very different faith and language and cultural circumstances, should have taken rank among the greatest writers of English. There is nothing like it in history. To read or to listen to Mrs. Naidu, the Begam Shah Nawaz, Dr. Tagore, Sir Akbar Hydari, Sir C. V. Raman, Sir Ross Masood, Mr. V. S. Srinivasa Sastri, Mr. Abdulla Yusuf Ali, Sir Jagadis Bose, Moulana Shaukat Ali, Sir T. B. Sapru or Sir Mohammed Iqbal is an experience that is full of the happiest promise for the world. And there are hundreds more, not to speak of the thousands of young men and women all over India who are using English daily, not because circumstances compel them to do so, but because they turn to it as a means of expression of the higher aspirations—the power working within them.

They know, too, that mastery in English means a very hard discipline; or it is perhaps only the English teacher of his own tongue who realises what this discipline costs and means in India. We who work in Indian schools and colleges do not wonder that an Indian triumphs in chess, in mathematics, in chemistry or physics, in logic and in spiritual fields, for we know of what extremes of self-sacrifice Indian personality is capable. It is part and parcel of that determination which has enabled Indian youths to lead the world in the exacting game of hockey and to win distinction in so many other kinds of sport.

This book, though so small, will bear out these things far better than I can express them, and it should provide encouragement to many young students who have little opportunity of possessing models of the best English written by their own countrymen and women. It is still, unfortunately, very difficult to obtain the writings of some of the greatest of Indian masters of English. And in this connection I may perhaps be allowed to suggest that in every larger educational institution in India there should be kept copies of the prose and verse of, say, thirty of the best of such writers.

A great deal of Indian work that is being recorded in English is far above the scope of this book, alike in philosophy and the physical sciences. But I am very pleased to include, by the kindness of Sir J. C. Bose, an example of the writing of a great Indian scientist. The investigations of the other Indian Fellows of the Royal Society, Sir C. V. Raman and Prof. Saha, are only intelligible to specialists. But they can all be brought into the generalization of one of the greatest of poets writing in English, the Irishman Mr. George Russell better known as A. E., who himself owes so much to the *Gita* :

> There were Indian sages who taught that the will when concentrated had a mastery which extended from the atomic to the infinite.

E. E. SPEIGHT

I

SHRIMATI RAMABAI RANADE

By Miss Susie Sorabji

The following beautiful tribute to a noble Indian lady reveals the sympathetic spirit of the writer on every page. The life of Miss Susie Sorabji has been written by her sister Miss Cornelia Sorabji.

Ramabai Ranade the founder and president of the now famous Seva Sadan of Poona, was born in a little hill-girt town, in the Satara district, of a family whose faithful service to the Peshwas had won for them a *jagir* in Devarashtra.

We picture the little Brahmin maiden, sitting on her father's knee, listening wide-eyed to his stories of saints and gods, and spirits, or watching her mother who was skilled in the knowledge of herbs and plants, distilling remedies for the villagers who came to her to be cured of their ills.

It was in such a wholesome unselfish atmosphere that Ramabai learned her first lessons of love for her fellow-men. No wonder that Justice Ranade found in her an apt pupil, when he began to prepare her (the little thirteen-year old bride, whom he had been compelled by his father to wed) for this great work that she was to do in Poona, after his death—a work that stands to-day a magnificent monument, showing what a good woman can achieve, if she will but yield herself, a willing instrument, to God's Omnipotent Hand.

We have illuminating glimpses of Ramabai Ranade's early life, in her *Reminiscences*—one such is peculiarly interesting. Her father was going to Poona—that wonderful town of which he used to bring home great stories to amuse his little daughter, as they sat under the shade of the dark trees in the hot afternoons, or beneath the feathery bamboos when the harvest moon rode high in the cloudless sky. For very long Ramabai had coveted a doll, a beautiful doll, such as he told her was to be purchased in the wonder-shops patronized by English people. Now she ventured, as he bade her goodbye, to whisper her wish to him, and obtained a ready promise that when he returned he would bring her what she so desired. For days she went about hugging her delightful secret. At last, to make matters doubly sure, she thought she would breathe her hopes to the tutelary Deity of the house, when she did her morning *pooja*. No one else should know about it! Oh no, it must be a secret between her father, herself and Shiva the Omnipotent, who was able to make her dream come true! So it was with a certain shock of surprise that she heard her brother say: 'So father is bringing a doll home for you!' 'How did you know?' asked the little maiden. Was it possible—but no it could not be!—the silent Shiva would never have betrayed her! Seeing her mystification the teasing brother would not tell her that the simple explanation of her puzzle was a letter he had received from his father, that morning. It is natural incidents like this that help us to see why Mrs. Ranade understood children so well, and was so loved by them. She never forgot, when with them, that she had once been a child, and so their little troubles and joys were always shared with a sympathy that was as natural to her, as it is rare with others.

When Justice Ranade decided to educate his girl-wife he set himself a task in which he had many opponents in his own household. From the time Ramabai, in the sanctuary of her learned husband's own room, made her first obeisance to the god of learning (Ganesh), to the day when she made her first speech before Sir James Fergusson, the Governor of Bombay, in the town Hall, in Poona, regarding the necessity of establishing a High School for Indian girls, she had to suffer quiet but bitter persecution, from the orthodox old women in her own house. But she allowed nothing to deter her from the course her husband had laid down for her. The bitter taunts she heard, downstairs, could not damp the joy she felt as she sat upstairs, and recited Sanskrit *shloks*, or read Meadows Taylor's thrilling *Tara* or *Sita* aloud to the Judge. What did it matter if, after a joyous afternoon at one of Pandita Ramabai's lectures, on coming home she was outcasted, so to speak, and not allowed to help in the kitchen work with the women of the family, until she had had a bath of purification? Even the water for the bath had to be drawn (so said the scandalized ladies) from a well outside, not from the fountain within the sacred precincts of their home. Patiently the brave-hearted girl, bent on learning all her husband wished her to know, and on attaining his ideal of an educated wife, pursued her course,—unmurmuringly. Quietly would she pick up the brass or copper vessel given to her, and go out to the dark well to draw water for the ablutions that would fit her to sit amongst her women relations again.

But this dark water brought on a fever which confined her to her bed for many a day. Then it was that Justice Ranade discovered all that she had been enduring, and put his foot down on the petty persecutions that had been going on, under his own roof, of the little girl-wife.

One cannot help thinking that it was thus that Ramabai Ranade learned the lesson of tolerance, and acquired that broadmindedness and sympathy which so fitted her for the presidentship of an institution that aims at giving to Indian women every opportunity for self-realisation and self-expression, and helps them to develop every God-given faculty. In the bracing atmosphere of her Seva Sadan she was able to give to her countrywomen what the human soul craves so ardently, and what is, in fact, its birthright.

Happy days, however, were in store for her—the Judge was appointed to Nasik, and there, at last, Ramabai had the joy of managing her own house. The golden memories, stored up in those days, helped immeasurably in brightening the dreariness of the ones that followed her husband's death. Whether in the house attending to the duties that every wife loves to perform, the duties that constitute the mysterious art of home-making (and are of an intellectual as much as of a social character), or in the garden which she so loved, where she coaxed the fragrant *mogra* or the stately rose to grow, Ramabai's heart sang merrily.

She used to tell how, when the Judge, in order to test her practical knowledge, asked her what sum she needed for the household monthly expenses, she who had never been allowed in Poona to know anything of the inner working of the domestic arrangements, named a figure below what was actually needed, and how, as the end of the month approached, when it hardly seemed possible that the little sum would last out the time, she was overcome with anxiety and shame, because she feared the emptiness of the household exchequer was due to her lack of economy. She would not speak, however, of the trouble, and tried to eke out the sum, till the true state of affairs was discovered by the kind Judge who assured her she had done splendidly, and that he had only been waiting for her to ask him for more money. The next household budget was, you may be sure, more accurately and more generously drawn up.

In Nasik, where some of the happiest days of her life were spent, Ramabai found a family that seemed a link between the old orthodox world that had tried to hold so tyrannical a sway over her, and the new progressive world that was beckoning to her to come and taste the joys of freedom, education, culture and reform. This family were keenly interested in social service, and, encouraged by their example, Ramabai began taking part in activities that had the good of others as their object. She presided at a school prizegiving, about this time, and was much interested in the school-children to whom she distributed the prizes.

But life is made up of sunshine and shadow, and the clouds gathered over Ramabai's horizon, when Justice Ranade in the course of his duties contracted cholera in a cholera-infected district. In a public resthouse the faithful young wife nursed him. Who can describe the agony of mind through which she passed in that lonely vigil by the sick man's bed. The local doctor declared his pulse was failing, and in her anguish she felt she must seek comfort in prayer, and so she stole out into the gathering darkness and made her way into the little temple in the courtyard, where sad and weary pilgrims for scores of years had sought and found relief in their despair, bowing, not surely as much to the little stone image there, as to the great God Who bids us seek His face, and to Whom the heavy-laden, stretching forth imploring hands into the darkness, cry: 'Have mercy on me!' There, in the dimly lighted temple, the weeping woman fell prostrate and poured out her heart to Him Who alone could help her, and felt a sudden peace within her soul. Somehow she knew her prayer had been answered, and she stole back to her post at the sick man's side, comforted and strengthened. Mr. Ranade recovered, and it was not till 1901 that he passed away.

Smitten, and well nigh overwhelmed, Ramabai shut herself up for a little; but then came the thought of the suffering womanhood around her, and it was in that temporary seclusion that she consecrated her life to the service of her countrywomen. Forgetting, or rather laying aside, her own sorrow, she went forth to minister to others in like trouble and to lift their eyes to the great fields of labour, the golden harvest of opportunity that awaited their sickles. New vistas opened before them, where hitherto there had been nothing but a blank wall. Yes, to these hopeless and despairing ones, she, like her friend Pandita Ramabai, came with a message of hope, of possibilities of service and usefulness, and bade them rise, and follow her. Together they ministered to the captive women in prison, to whom she took the sympathy and cheer they so much needed to keep them from despair. They visited the little lads in the Reformatory, who were being given a chance to make good, and fit themselves for honest citizenship. Nor was the bedside of the sick and dying forgotten; and the hospital where lived the mentally afflicted ones. Around her she gathered a band of women who used to meet, week by week, to listen to lectures on how to render First Aid to the injured, to work for the poor, and to hear accounts of women in other lands who served their fellows.

Where did she dream that beautiful dream of a Home of Service, where would come as helpers all those whose hearts God had touched with love for the great suffering world? One cannot tell; perhaps as she sat at the feet of her husband, that prince of reformers, listening to his inspiring words; or in those dark days, when a simple English or Sanskrit lesson was taken in her husband's room; or when attendance at a lecture given by her friend Pandita Ramabai would bring down a storm of opposition and reproach. At any rate the dream became a reality, and one wonderful day, she formulated her plans, organized the work which has grown, so marvellously, into the colossal Institution, known as the Poona Seva Sadan, with its branches all over the Presidency of Bombay.

How does the mighty oak grow from the little acorn? Who can follow the miraculous process? One can only watch, and wonder and rejoice.

As early as 1904, at the All-India Women's Conference, in Bombay, Mrs. Ranade outlined the nature of the social service she proposed should be carried on by those whose motto, she declared, was to be: 'Life is a Sacred Trust'. How fully she herself realized her trusteeship, every dav of her selfless life proved.

The great Seva Sadan had its inaugural meeting in Mrs. Ranade's own house (that home where her husband had brought the girl-wife whom he was to train for service). From a small attempt on the part of the members of 'The Hindu Ladies' Social and Literary Club' to educate women by means of regular classes and institutions, started to impart instruction of a religious, literary, medical and industrial character, the work gradually grew into the splendid organization it is, and was at the time of Mrs. Ranade's death.

In a brief review, written by her ten years after she began, she set forth some of the principal objects of the Seva Sadan. These are :—

(*a*) To teach and educate women by means of regular classes and to impart instruction of a religious, literary, scientific, medical and industrial character. To teach them the principles of First Aid, Hygiene, Sanitation and Domestic Economy.

(*b*) To widen the range of women's knowledge by means of libraries, lectures, publications, books, magazines etc., and by tours, excursions, and other popular methods.

(*c*) To enable women to participate intelligently in all domestic, social and national responsibilities, and to inculcate in their minds the principles of self-reliance and mutual helpfulness.

(*d*) To train women to render, in a patriotic spirit, educational, medical and philanthropic service to the motherland, and to their brothers and sisters in specially backward areas.

(*e*) To help in the promotion of national work in all

these and similar ways, for the social, material and educational uplift of Indian women.

(*f*) To promote greater fellowship amongst the women of India.

(*g*) To start institutions for the promotion of these objects and ideals, and to affiliate those that are working for them.

(*h*) To adopt such measures as will be conducive to the furtherance of these objects.

(*i*) To work directly to promote the all-round well-being of Indian womanhood.

Everyone of these objects, this brave worker kept in view throughout the fifteen years she presided over the destiny of this institution.

One of Mrs. Ranade's greatest achievements was the establishment of the Seva Sadan Nursing and Medical Associations. It was due to her inspiration, and influence alone, that high caste Hindu widows and girls volunteered to take up a work that, above all others, is crying out to be done in India. What marvellous forces she was harnessing for the service of the women and children of India when she took her first batch of probationers to the Sassoon Hospital Nursing Department, even Mrs. Ranade did not know! But all through the coming years, there will be a stream of women pouring into the hospitals, to be equipped for service to the suffering women and girls of this land. It was her hand that unlocked the door that will, and must remain open, as long as there are pain and suffering in our land.

The ordinary social worker, surveying the field of work before her, might easily have been discouraged, but Mrs. Ranade's incurable optimism saw no obstacles—saw indeed only the greatest opportunities for service and seized them. There was hardly a phase of work to which she and her workers did not turn their attention. To the home, with its wide open doors, came widows, who sought hope and comfort, and found it in serving others; young girls with aims and hopes, and a longing to fit themselves for a wider life; little children who needed protection and love; the sick and sorrowful who claimed aid and advice. For all and sundry the Seva Sadan had help, and to all Mrs. Ranade, the loving mother and sympathizer, opened her heart. In the world of education, her help was claimed in text book and similar committees; she was the leader in Poona of an agitation for compulsory primary education for girls. Her reputation as a writer was established by the production of her book *Reminiscences*, now regarded as a Marathi classic.

In politics, the versatility of this wonderful woman was evidenced when she threw herself heart and soul into the campaign begun to obtain the vote for Indian women. Surely a new era dawned for India, when she presided over a gigantic meeting of women who crowded (twenty or thirty deep) round the courtyard of the Seva Sadan, up to the second or third story and even on the roof, to listen in rapt silence to the eloquent speeches of those, who, like their western sisters, were awakened to their duties and privileges as citizens.

Sir H. Lawrence, a member of the Executive Council, declared at the excited debate on the question of women's suffrage, that he would consider it an honour to serve on a Council of which Mrs. Ramabai Ranade was a member.

She anticipated members of Council who to-day are introducing bills regarding a widow's title to her husband's property, by organizing lectures and debates in order to educate public opinion to demand the alteration of the law to suit present-day conditions. Before she could accomplish much, however, she died.

A few years before her death, she was asked by the Poona Municipality to undertake the care of the thousands of women pilgrims and their little children, who attended the Annual Fair at Alandi. With her faithful band of workers, who seemed, from the very first, to have caught her spirit of love and devotion, she set forth for the sacred place, and there in the temple courtyard, day and night, she and her co-workers stood, organizing the women's visits to the shrine, taking charge of the infants while some weary pilgrim slipped in, to lay her offerings and her prayers at the feet of the god. Through the hot days, they would deal out cool draughts of water to the poor thirsty ones, and so really and materially did they improve the condition of these countless frightened hordes of women, that they came and fell at Mrs. Ranade's feet in gratitude for the very real help rendered them.

Since her initiation of this great branch of Social Work, the Seva Sadan has been asked to work in co-operation with the Provincial Committee in organizing National Health, and Baby Sections, in the Exhibition that is held by the Municipality, for the benefit of the pilgrims that flock to Alandi from all over India.

One of her outstanding characteristics was her inability to see that there was anything extraordinary in her undertakings. Some one said to her one day: 'Dear Mrs. Ranade, how wonderful it is, that you should be able to do so much, and such great things for God!' 'Oh no!' she exclaimed quickly, 'there is nothing wonderful in what I am doing. I was fortunate in being the instrument that happened to be lying nearest God's Hand; and so He picked me up, and used me!' 'There lies the secret,' answered her friend, 'It is because you lie so near His Hand that He uses you.'

Soon after her husband's death, when in her utter misery she shut herself up for a little, there went to her an English friend, one who was sure that the only consolation for Mrs. Ranade lay in consoling others. 'Come with me', she said, 'and let us carry a ray of sunshine to those who are shut out, alas, by their own wrongdoing, from the world'. And so she carried her off to the captive women in Yeravada Jail. With that wonderful gift of sympathy that she possessed in such limitless measure, this good woman became the 'prison angel' to these unfortunate women, throwing herself, heart and soul, into the work she continued so faithfully for over twenty years.

Nothing deterred her from those fortnightly visits to the jail, not the length and loneliness of the drive out there nor yet the apparent hopelessness of the task before her. Summer or winter, rain or shine, her brougham used to be seen driving up to the big iron gates, behind which were so many miserable sin-burdened souls. Her gentle sympathetic inquiries about their health and comfort soon drew a crowd of women round her; and then, when they had all gathered, generally about two hundred, in the open courtyard, she would read aloud a passage of Tukaram's, which she would translate into simple language, explaining the uplifting thoughts and sentiments, to those who had wandered so far—so very far—alas, from the path of righteousness. And as she read, into the hard faces would steal a softness as new as it was beautiful, and eyes, unused to tears, would grow moist and wistful, as new thoughts and aspirations and longings were aroused by the gentle pleading of the one whose visits made the prison less dismal, and their lot less intolerable

Is it surprising that away in far-off Africa a dying Indian woman on being told she could not live much longer, gathered her new-born babe to her breast, and made up her mind, in her agony of fear, to cross the (to her) terrible ocean, in order to lay it in the motherly arms of her friend Ramabai Ranade? How faithfully she tended the helpless infant, till the boy grew to manhood, is a story by itself.

Then came the end. It was a hot April afternoon, when the Angel of Death hovered over the chamber where the great woman lay dying. For some days she had been ill—in agony, but oh so brave, so uncomplaining, so calm, even to the very end thinking of others rather than of herself. It was not, however, till the western sun had dipped behind the Ghats, and the sudden darkness of the oriental night had settled down upon the crowded city, that her soul took its flight to God.

They laid her in the large hall that bore her name—a noble beautiful figure she lay there, wrapped in her snow-white draperies, and covered with the fragrant roses and *mogras* she had loved so well to weave into garlands to adorn the life-sized portrait of her husband, that always held the place of honour in her simple room.

The news of her passing soon spread through the city and they came, one and all,—men, women and children—an endless procession, to file in silent reverence past her who had been a mother to her people, Ramabai, the friend, the enthusiast, the worker. She had spent her years in the uplifting of her people—She had blazed the trail for them in a practically trackless wild!—Who, who would follow her? Thank God, there are many—many noble women, from her own dearly loved Seva-Sadan, who have taken up the torch her dying hands dropped, who are now carrying on the glorious work she started and who are adding to their ranks every day, devoted, well-equipped, enthusiastic workers whose one object in life is to strive for the uplift and betterment of suffering humanity.

NOTES

P. 2, ll. 1-2. If she will only give herself up willingly into Almighty God's hand, for Him to use her for His work.

Illuminating glimpses: glimpses of her early life, which throw light upon her nature and character.

Reminiscences: memories.

Wonder-shops . . . people: shops full of wonderful things, where the English people used to buy what they needed.

Tutelary Deity: guardian god or goddess.

Mystification: bewilderment. To *mystify* a person means to puzzle him or to say something he cannot understand.

Sanctuary: a sacred place, a place where one can be safe from any trouble.

Obeisance: a bowing down in reverence or salutation.

Orthodox: believing aright.

Philip Meadows Taylor: (1806-1876) An Englishman who served the Nizam of Hyderabad with much distinction from 1826 to 1860. He wrote a number of books containing vivid and exciting accounts of Indian life, including *Confessions of a Thug* (1839), *Tippoo Sultan* (1840), *Tara* (1863), *Seeta* (1873), and *The Story of my Life* (1877).

Scandalized: shocked.

Precincts: Space within the boundaries of a building or place.

P. 4, § 2. An institution which gives Indian women every chance to develop their own powers which God has given them, by actually taking part in social life."

Pandita Ramabai: An Indian lady born in a village of the Western Ghats, the daughter of a learned Shastri. She herself became proficient in Sanskrit. Her husband died leaving her with a little child and in poor circumstances, but by writing a book she made money for her passage to England, where she studied at Cheltenham College, and published a book, *The High Caste Hindu Woman.* Then she went to America where she made money by her lectures and writings. Returning to India she opened a home for high-caste girls and widows, the Sharada Sadan, in Bombay. Later, after much noble work among famine sufferers, she organized the Mukti Sadan, at Khedgaon, near Poona. This developed into a school with nearly two thousand pupils, of whom over four hundred were in the Kindergarten, a Training School for Teachers and an Industrial School, all directed by this wonderful little lady, whose life was spent half in prayer and half in the management of her House of Salvation. She died in 1922.

Bracing: strengthening. So we speak of bracing air: air which makes one feel eager to do one's work.

Mogra: the jasmine or jessamine.

Household budget: accounts of household expenses.

Consecrated her life . . . : regarded it as sacred to. . . .

Sickles: short curving knives for cutting corn.

Vistas: views, scenes.

Reformatory: a place where bad children are trained to be good citizens.

Colossal: very large.

Acorn: the seed of the oak-tree.

Inaugural meetings: first meetings. To inaugurate: to begin; inauguration is a solemn beginning of something.

P. 9, l. 32. Mrs. Ranade was an optimist, that is she always hoped for the best; it was incurable, that is it was part of her nature to be hopeful, and could not be changed.

Agitation: a strong movement to support something.

Compulsory education: education which people were *compelled* to let their children enjoy.

Versatility: to be versatile means to be able to turn to many things and do them well.

Rapt silence: a silence of devoted attention.

P. 10, l. 31. By educating the public by holding lectures and debates she prepared them to demand an alteration of the law regarding the right of a widow to her husband's property. This she did before any members of Council tried to make changes in the law.

QUESTIONS

1. What does Miss Sorabji tell us about the childhood of Ramabai?

2. What were the difficulties Ramabai had to face as a young wife?

3. In what ways did her life become happier after the removal to Nasik?
4. What were the objects for which Mrs. Ranade organized the Poona Seva Sadan?
5. What were Mrs. Ranade's services to Indian medical work?
6. What was the work Mrs. Ranade carried on at the Alandi annual Fair?
7. What anecdote does Miss Sorabji tell illustrating the humility of Mrs. Ranade?
8. Describe the experiences of Mrs. Ranade in Yeravada Jail.
9. Give a brief summary of the work accomplished by Mrs Ranade.

SUBJECTS FOR ESSAYS

1. Women and Public Life in India.
2. The Meaning of Patriotism To-Day.
3. The Good Points of the Old Orthodox Customs.
4. The Value of Social Service.
5. The Characteristics of Indian Womanhood.
6. Describe any Social Institution with which you are acquainted and give an account of its activities.
7. The Influence of a Good Woman.

II

FRANÇOIS BERNIER IN INDIA (1659-1667)

BY ABDULLA YUSUF ALI, C.B.E.

Mr. Abdulla Yusuf Ali, C.B.E., M.A., L.L.M. is a distinguished retired civilian who divides his affection between law, politics, literature and the study of art. He passed into the Indian Civil Service with a brilliant record, and has served both the Indian Government and that of H.E.H. the Nizam of Hyderabad, and has been principal of the Islamia College in Lahore. For some years he has resided in England, writing for the higher public organs and associated with the work of the League of Nations. He has written and lectured much on Islamic subjects, and served on the Punjab University Commission. He has utilized his administrative experience and his scholarship in writing his well known book *The Making of India,* in which he outlines in a most readable way the different elements, geographical, ethical, natural, moral and political, that went to the building up of the Indian people. The following piece is taken from his school text-book entitled *Three Travellers to India,* the other two travellers being the Chinese pilgrim Yuan Chwang, and the Arab Sheikh Ibn Batuta.

FRANÇOIS BERNIER was born in 1620, of French parents who were cultivators of the soil. He received a good education, and travelled between the ages of 27 and 30 in Germany, Poland, Switzerland and Italy. This opened up his mind and laid the foundations for that taste for wider travel which eventually took him to the East. He took his degree as Doctor of Medicine in 1652 in the University of Montpelier in the south of France. A visit to Palestine and Syria in 1654 brought him into contact with the Ottoman Empire. His judgment on that Empire and on the East generally is not favourable. As a good Catholic, he seems to have had a bad opinion of Islam. Between 1656 and 1658 he visited Egypt and the Red Sea ports of Arabia. From Mocha, well-known for its export of coffee, he took an Indian ship to Surat, which was then the principal Indian port for Arabia. He seems to have arrived in India early in 1659.

Bernier started on his way to the capital (Delhi) from Surat, and got as far as Ahmedabad. That city was in a state of turmoil. The vanquished prince Dara was within a day's journey, and Ahmedabad had shut its gates against him for fear of Aurangzeb. The prince was in great straits. On the one hand, the governors and officials gave him no encouragement. On the other, the country was full of freebooters of the Koli tribe, an aboriginal forest race inhabiting the outskirts of Gujrat. They hung round his camp, ready to rob and murder. To crown his misfortunes, one of the ladies of the prince's household fell ill. By a strange chance Bernier encountered the camp as he was going up north. The prince wanted a physician, and offered him the protection of his camp, such as it was, against the murderous attentions of the Kolis. Bernier remained with him a few days. But the position in the camp itself was dangerous. The bad news from Ahmedabad soon arrived, that the Governor of the city had declared himself unfriendly to Dara.

The rest of the scene may be described in the philosopher's own words. 'It was at the break of day that the Governor's message was delivered, and the shrieks of the females drew forth tears from every eye. We were all overwhelmed with confusion and dismay, gazing in speechless horror at each other, at a loss what plan to recommend, and ignorant of the fate which perhaps awaited us from hour to hour. We observed Dara stepping out more dead than alive, speaking now to one, then to another; stopping and consulting even the commonest soldier. He saw great fear in every countenance, and felt assured that he would be left without a single follower. But what was to become of him? Whither must he go? To delay his departure was to hasten his ruin.

'During the time that I remained in the prince's retinue we marched, nearly without intermission, day and night; and so insupportable was the heat, and so suffocating the dust, that of the three large oxen of Gujrat which drew my carriage, one had died, another was in a dying stage, and the third was unable to proceed from fatigue. Dara felt anxious to retain me in his service, especially as one of his wives had a bad wound in her leg; yet neither his threats nor entreaties could procure for me a single horse, ox, or camel; so completely had he lost power and influence.

'I remained behind, therefore, because of the absolute impossibility of continuing the journey, and could not but weep when I beheld the prince depart with a force diminished to four or five hundred horsemen. There were also a couple of elephants, laden, it was said, with gold and silver . . . . . I could not cherish the hope that the prince would succeed in crossing the sandy desert . . . . In fact nearly the whole of the men, and many of the women, did perish; some dying of thirst, hunger, or fatigue, while others were killed by the hands of the merciless Kolis. Happy would it have been for Dara, had he not himself survived this perilous march!'

Here we must leave the unfortunate prince Dara, and proceed with Bernier's own experience with the Kolis.

Though a philosopher, he had to use an ordinary man's wiles to excite their compassion and keep what little money he had about his person. 'I made a grand display,' he says, 'of my professional skill; and my two servants, who experienced the same terror as myself, declared that I was the most eminent physician in the world, and that Dara's soldiers had used me extremely ill, robbing me of everything valuable. It was fortunate for me that we succeeded in creating in these people an interest in my favour; for after detaining me seven or eight days, they attached a bullock to my carriage, and conducted me within view of the minarets of Ahmedabad.'

In this city he met a Mughal nobleman who was proceeding to Delhi. He now travelled under his protection. On the way up through the desert of Rajputana, they saw dead men, elephants, oxen, horses, and camels,—pitiful wrecks of what had been Dara's army.

Bernier reached Delhi within seven weeks of leaving Surat,—a distance of 800 miles. By this time his money was nearly exhausted, and he was glad to accept an allowance from the Mughal Court. He calls this a salary in his capacity as a physician. But as he seems to have filled no office or post under Aurangzeb, it was really in the nature of an allowance for hospitality, such as was usually made to distinguished strangers according to the traditions of the Mughal Court. He also got another 'salary' of the same nature from a nobleman and high official at the Court. This amounted to three hundred rupees per month. But the cost of provisions in Delhi was so high that he would almost have starved if he had depended on that allowance alone. He could not help recalling the fact that in France he could have lived, on half a rupee per day, on as good food as the king himself.

The nobleman to whom Bernier attached himself was Danishmand Khan, who had been originally a Persian merchant. He rose in the Mughal service to the high office of Bakhshi (paymaster of the forces), and the rank of Panjhazari (Commander of five thousand horse). Aurangzeb appointed him Governor of Delhi. He seems also to have been Secretary of State for Foreign Affairs, and to have enjoyed his sovereign's confidence. Bernier calls him 'the most learned man of Asia, ... and one of the most powerful and distinguished . . . . Lords of the Court.' After devoting his mornings to his State duties, he used to set apart his afternoons to philosophical studies. In consideration of his studious habits and his work in the Foreign Department, he was released from the duty of appearing twice a day at the ceremony of saluting the king, which was compulsory for the other great noblemen of the Court. With the French traveller he eagerly read the works of Gassendi and Descartes, French philosophers who were then dead but whose works were at the height of their fame. Gassendi had personally taught Bernier, who had tended him on his death-bed. Descartes was the author of the Discourse on Method, which forms a landmark in the development of modern science and philosophy. Danishmand Khan also counted, among his favourite subjects of study, astronomy, geography, and anatomy. But his learning and his position in no way detracted from his lovable character. Bernier was much attached to him and always calls him affectionately 'My Agha' (My Lord).

There were other noblemen at Court who were interested in European learning. Fazl Khan, the Grand

Chamberlain of the Royal Household, asked Bernier to teach him the leading languages of Europe, and insisted upon being supplied with a select number of the best European books before he gave him permission to leave the Mughal Empire. Bernier, on the other hand, lived in India more like a student than a traveller. For the five or six years he was in the Mughal court his principal employment was to learn Persian, translate European works into that language (then the court language in India) and discourse systematically with the best Pandits on Hindu learning, religion, customs and institutions. He had a regular supply of books from Europe, and he collected in India books that interested him. He had formed the design (which he could not carry out) of translating a history of Kashmir from Persian into French.

In the spring of 1665 the court paid a visit to Kashmir, attended by a grand retinue, in which Bernier travelled with Danishmand Khan. As Bernier's pay was three hundred rupees a month, he was expected to keep two good Turkoman horses, and he also took with him a powerful Persian camel and driver, a groom for his horses, a cook, and a servant to go before his horse with a flagon of water in his hand, according to the custom of the country. It was slow and solemn marching, with a big camp, consisting of over three hundred thousand men,—practically a moving city. The distance between Delhi and Lahore is about three hundred miles, and was considered equivalent to fifteen days' journey. They took about two months in their leisurely march. The rivers were ordinarily unbridged, and were crossed on bridges of boats. The crossing often took several days. On the way there were large tracts of uncultivated land, covered with jungle. There were game preserves, and the huge royal party indulged in hunting as they went along. There was the chase of black buck with tame hunting chitahs. There was the Nilgai hunt, in which a net was first spread round a wide extent of country, and then drawn closer into a smaller and smaller circle until the riders and men were able to enter and kill the animals with arrows, short pikes, swords and muskets. There was also the hunting of cranes with hawks.

But the most honourable as well as the most dangerous hunt was that of the lion. This was reserved for the king and the princes. Lions were still found and hunted in this part of the country. The first step was to tie up an ass as a bait near the spot to which the gamekeepers had traced the lion's retreat. When there was a kill by night, the lion usually sought out water to quench his thirst, and retired again to sleep by day. After the bait had been taken several times and the lion had been definitely located, large nets were spread round the country and drawn closer and closer together, to narrow the circle. When the space was sufficiently manageable, the king appeared on an elephant protected in places with plates of iron, and attended by the grand master of the hunt, some noblemen mounted on elephants, and a great number of mace-bearers on horseback and of game-keepers on foot, armed with half-pikes. He immediately approached the net on the outside, and fired at the lion with a large musket. The wounded animal invariably made a spring at the elephant, but was arrested by the net. The king continued to fire until the lion was killed. As sport this sounds tame, and the chances at first sight seem to be all against the lion. In practice the lion often escaped over the net, as happened on the present occasion, and then the sport became most dangerous. When the lion was finally killed, he was accurately measured, and the details about his size, skin, teeth, and claws were carefully recorded in the royal archives.

At Lahore they waited for the melting of the snows in the passes that gave access to Kashmir. They followed the Pir Panjal route by way of Bhimbar. They had to cut down their baggage, and change their tents to smaller ones, suitable for the hill country. The heat was intense until they reached the hills, and there were many casualties on the march. The retinue of the king and the nobles was also very much curtailed. And yet it was estimated that the number of porters employed at Bhimbar was fifteen thousand. A royal order fixed their pay at twenty rupees for every 100 lbs. weight. The time or distance covered by this wage is not stated, but in any case it seems to have been on a very liberal scale, and we can understand the large number of volunteers who came of their own accord in order to earn money, in addition to those who were ordered up by authority.

As soon as they had climbed the Pir Panjal range, and begun the descent into the valley of Kashmir, there was a marvellous change in temperature and scenery. They were transported on a sudden from the torrid to the temperate zone. Bernier thought he was transferred from India to Europe. 'I almost imagined myself,' he says, 'in the mountains of Auvergne[1] in a forest of fir, oak, elm and plane trees, and could not avoid feeling strongly

[1] A plateau in the south of central France in the Departments of Puy de Dôme and Cantal.

the contrast between this scene and the burning fields of Hindustan, which I had just quitted and where nothing of the kind is seen.' A little further on, the two sides of the hill presented a striking contrast. The south side, that looking towards India, was full of Indian and European plants mingled together. The side exposed to the north was crowded exclusively with the flora of Europe. There was a riot of vegetable life. Hundreds of old trees were decaying or dead, and plunging into abysses down which man never ventured, while young trees were shooting out of the ground, to supply the places of the generations that were passing away.

The green and well-watered valley of Kashmir had the appearance of a fertile and highly cultivated garden. 'Meadows and vineyards, fields of rice, wheat, hemp, saffron, and many sorts of vegetables, among which are intermingled trenches filled with water, rivulets, canals, and several small lakes, vary the enchanting scene. The whole ground is gaily covered with our European flowers and plants, and covered with our apple, pear, plum, apricot, and walnut trees, all bearing fruit in great abundance. The private gardens are full of melons, water melons, and many vegetables and herbs with which we are unacquainted.' The fruit, thought the traveller, was inferior in quality and variety to that of France. But this was due not to any inferiority in soil or climate, 'but merely to the comparative ignorance of the gardeners, for they do not understand the culture and the grafting of trees as we do in France.'

The capital (Srinagar) is described in picturesque terms. It was built on the banks of fresh-water lakes formed of live springs and streams. The river (Jhelum) ran through the town, and was connected with the lakes by means of a canal wide enough to admit boats. Two wooden bridges spanned the river. The houses were of timber, well-built, with two or three storeys. Most of them had pretty little gardens, and many of them had canals with pleasure-boats, communicating with the lakes. The islands in the lakes were well laid out in delightful gardens, as were also the sides of the hills around, from which beautiful views could be obtained of the town, river, canals, lakes, islands and gardens. Then, as now, the Shalimar gardens, with their canals, fountains, summer-houses, poplar avenues, and carpets of emerald turf, made an unerring appeal to lovers of nature and art. The rivalry of Kashmiri and Mughal poets in their artificial exaggerations did not much impress the French philosopher. But he was free to confess that he was charmed with Kashmir, 'the Paradise of the Indies.' 'In truth,' he says, 'the kingdom surpasses in beauty all that my warm imagination had anticipated. It is probably unequalled by any country of the same extent.'

After this visit to Kashmir Bernier seems to have parted company with the Mughal court. In November 1665 he left Agra with the French jeweller Tavernier for Bengal. He found this province excelling Egypt in fertility. It produced rice in such abundance that it supplied not only neighbouring provinces but remote states. Sugar was another of its products much in demand, its exports going as far as Arabia and Persia. The Portuguese, who had many settlements on the delta of the Ganges and the adjacent coasts, had introduced special kinds of confectionery, in which there was a valuable trade. Cotton and silk textiles were also produced and exported in large quantities. The cheapness of provisions struck Bernier, as it had struck Ibn Batuta. Twenty or more good fowls could be purchased for a single rupee, and fish was abundant. Many of the European adventurers, Portuguese, English, and Dutch, resorted to this Province and settled down there: there was a saying current among them that there were a hundred gates open for entrance, but not one for departure.

From Bengal Bernier passed on to Southern India, and early in 1667 he made his way to Surat, from whence he took ship to Persia. Early in 1669 he returned to France, and in the following year he published his book and dedicated it to the French king. It passed through several editions. Soon after the publication of the first French edition, it was translated into English and Dutch, the respective languages of the two nations which were then contending for commercial supremacy in the East. He died in 1688, the year of the English Revolution.

The routine of the Mughal Court was frequently relieved by the reception of embassies. Those which Bernier saw came from such varied powers as the Usbek Khan of Turkestan, beyond the borders of Kabul province, the Dutch who had several factories in the Mughal dominions, the Sharif of Mecca, the King of Yemen, the Prince of Basra in Iraq, the King of Abyssinia, the Shah of Persia, and the King of Tibet. Each of these embassies brought appropriate presents from its own country and was given in return more costly presents by the Mughal Emperor. They were received with more or less distinction according to the show they made, and the estimate in which the sovereign they came from was held in the Mughal Court. The King of Tibet was treated as a tributary, and a treaty was arranged with him, which included among its terms a provision that the coins of Tibet should bear on one side an acknowledgment of Aurangzeb's suzerainty. Tibet was then on the trade route between India and China. The caravans started from Patna, passed through Lhassa, and penetrated to the Chinese frontier from the west.

Persia was a neighbouring and powerful kingdom; and its ambassadors were treated more or less alike in the Mughal court. As Persian was the court language in India, the Persians were at home with the Mughals, and many were the combats of wit that were exchanged, according to the common gossip of Delhi. Aurangzeb himself observed strict formality in diplomatic intercourse. But Bernier heard of many jokes exchanged by Shah Jahan with the Persian ambassador of his day. Shah Abbas was the Persian monarch then, and his ambassador did not hesitate, in convivial gatherings, to repay Shah Jahan in his own coin. Shah Jahan once, in a fit of annoyance, tried to snub the ambassador by asking: 'Has then Shah Abbas no gentleman in his court that he sends me such a fool?' 'Oh yes!' replied the Persian ambassador: 'the court of my sovereign abounds with men far more polite and accomplished than I am, but he adapts the ambassador to the king!'

Another instance of a quick repartee may be quoted. Shah Jahan had invited the Persian ambassador to dinner. The monarch was partial to the homely dish of *khichri*, and was doing full justice to it, when he saw the Persian busy picking bones in his dish. Said the monarch sarcastically: 'Elchi Ji! (my lord ambassador), what shall the dogs eat?' '*Khichri*!' was the prompt and crushing reply.

In contrast with these frivolous witticisms picked up from the petty talk of the court, Bernier records a scathing speech on education addressed by Aurangzeb to his old teacher. ' Show me a well-educated youth,' said Aurangzeb, ' and I will say that it is doubtful who has the stronger claim to his gratitude, his father or his tutor. You taught me that the whole of Feringhistan was no more than some inconsiderable island . . . whose monarchs resembled petty Rajas, and that the potentates of Hindustan eclipsed the glory of all other kings; . . . and that Persia, Usbek, Kashgar, Tartary, and Cathay, Pegu, Siam, Chin, and Ma-chin, trembled at the name of the king of the Indies. Admirable geographer! deeply-read historian! Was it not the duty of my teacher to make me acquainted with the distinguishing features of every nation of the earth: its resources and strength; its mode of warfare, its manners, religion, forms of government, and wherein its interests principally consist; and, by a regular course of historical reading, to render me familiar with the origin of States, their progress, and decline; the events, accidents, or errors owing to which such great changes and mighty revolutions have been effected? Far from having given me a full and deep knowledge of the history of mankind, scarcely did I learn from you the names of my ancestors, the renowned founders of this empire.

' You kept me in total ignorance of their lives, of the events which preceded, and the extraordinary talents that enabled them to achieve their extensive conquests. A familiarity with the language of surrounding nations may be indispensable in a king, but you would teach me to read and write Arabic; doubtless conceiving that you placed me under an everlasting obligation for sacrificing so large a portion of my time to the study of a language wherein no one can hope to become proficient without ten or twelve years of close application. Forgetting how many important subjects ought to be embraced in the education of a prince, you acted as if it were chiefly necessary that he should possess great skill in grammar, and such knowledge as belongs to a doctor of law; and thus did you waste the precious hours of my youth in the dry, unprofitable, and never ending task of learning words!'

The city of Delhi which Bernier saw was the same city which we now see within the walls, the city of Shah Jahan. He did not think much of the fortifications, nor of the size of the city, but the suburbs were extensive, and had good gardens and open spaces. The population of Delhi (he thought) was perhaps equal to that of Paris. The Fort contained the palace, which commanded a view of the river. The sandy space between the river and the palace was used for reviews of troops and for elephant fights. The works in the Fort itself were by no means strong; in his opinion a battery of moderate force would soon level them with the ground. There were two principal streets running in a straight line, with brick houses and shops on either side, and five smaller streets not so long or straight. The rest were narrow alleys built without regard to symmetry. The poorer houses were built of mud and thatch, and fires were frequent, resulting in much loss of life. He considered Delhi a mere collection of many villages, or a military camp with only a few more conveniences than are usually found in such camps.

The better houses were fairly roomy, with court-yards, gardens, fountains, terraces, and underground chambers.

to which the inmates retired for coolness from noon till four or five o'clock in the afternoon. Some had *Khas Khanas*, or small pavilions made of *khas*, the fragrant root which is still used in the hot weather for *khas* screens (tattis). The floor of a rich man's house was usually covered with a cotton mattress four inches thick, to give a soft tread to the feet. Over the mattress was spread a fair white cloth in the summer, and a silk carpet in the winter. One or two mattresses were placed to make the seats of honour, covered with embroidery in silk, gold, and silver. On this sat the host and any distinguished guests that came on a visit. They leaned their backs on large cushions of brocade, and other cushions were placed round the room for guests not quite so high in the social scale. Five or six feet above the floor, the walls were full of niches, in which were placed porcelain vases and flower-pots by way of ornaments. The ceiling was gilt and painted in arabesque with no figures of men or animals.

The shops were not decked out in the showy way characteristic of Europe. Provisions were dear and not very good. A lover of good cheer, thought Bernier, was not likely to quit Paris to visit Delhi. Here, unless a man was of the highest rank, he must live miserably. The streets abounded in astrologers and fortune-tellers. The artisans were not without skill, but they were despised, treated with harshness, and paid insufficiently for their labour. Their occupations were hereditary, and no one aspired to rise from the condition of life in which he was born.

The two principal public buildings in Delhi apart from the Fort, were the Jami Mosque, which still stands, and the Begam Sarai, which was destroyed in the Mutiny. The mosque was situated on high ground. Its three great domes and its minarets were of white marble. The rest of the building was of red stone, easy to work but liable to peel off in flakes from the effects of time.

The king went to this mosque every Friday in public procession. The *sarai* had been built by Shah Jahan's eldest daughter Jahan-Ara. It was in the form of a large courtyard with series of rooms opening out of a handsome verandah. Rich foreign merchants came here to stay and store their goods. The gate were closed at night, and there was perfect security from thefts. Bernier wished that a score of similar structures were erected in Paris for foreign merchants.

Agra was an older city than Delhi of Shah Jahan, and had been more in favour as a royal residence before the days of Aurangzeb. In essentials its character was the same as that of Delhi, but it was larger in extent, it had a larger number of the better class residences built of stone or brick, and its *sarais* were finer and more numerous. But it was not so well designed as Delhi, and it was not defended by walls. Its surroundings, however, presented a greener aspect from the multitude of trees and gardens. The Jesuits had a church and college in this city, and the Dutch a factory. The chief architectural monuments of Agra were Akbar's Tomb and the Taj Mahal. To the Frenchman, who looked upon the East as 'semi-barbarous,' it was an astounding experience to gaze on the faultless beauty of the Taj. In spite of himself he allows his words to assume a tone of enthusiasm unusual to him. 'The edifice,' he says, 'has a magnificent appearance, and is conçeived and executed effectually. Nothing offends the eye; on the contrary, it is delighted with every part and never tired with looking. The last time I visited this mausoleum, I was in the company of a French merchant, who, as well as myself, thought that this extraordinary fabric could not be sufficiently admired. I did not venture to express my opinion, fearing that my taste might have become corrupted by my long residence in the Indies, and as my companion was come recently from France, it was quite a relief to my mind to hear him say that he had seen nothing in Europe so bold and majestic.'

NOTES

(The word François is pronounced something like *Frahnswah*. The little mark under the Ç means that *c* is pronounced like *s*).

The Ottoman Empire: Ottoman means Turkish. It is the same word as Osman or Othman, the name of the founder of a Turkish dynasty.
Flagon: large earthenware bottle.
Bait: food to tempt an animal to come near and be caught.
Mace-bearers: a mace is a staff of office, generally carried before a king.
Archives: government records.
Casualties: accidents or deaths.
Abysses: very deep places.
Grafting: putting a portion of one tree into the stem of another, to improve the quality of the fruit.
Poplar: a tall, slender, dark tree.
Confectionery: cakes and sweets. A man who makes and sells them is called a confectioner.
Annoyance: *annoy* is a word commonly used. We say: 'I hope the children will not annoy you', and: 'How annoying it is to be late for school!'
Khichri: a dish consisting of rice and lentils.
Feringistan: Europe. **Usbek:** Khan of Turkestan.
Niches: hollows.
Cathay: North China. **Chin:** South China. **Machin:** Mongolia and Chinese Turkestan.
Artisans: workers in various crafts.

Jesuits: Members of the famous Society of Jesus, a Roman Catholic society which sent well-trained missionaries to all parts of the world to preach and teach.
Mausoleum: a royal tomb of imposing grandeur.

QUESTIONS

1. Tell in a few words the story of Bernier's experience with Prince Dara.
2. What does the author say of the abilities of the governor of Delhi?
3. Describe the lion-hunt on the way to Lahore.
4. What does Bernier say of the following?
   (*a*) The Valley of Kashmir.
   (*b*) Srinagar.
   (*c*) Bengal.
5. What were the Embassies which came to the Mughal Court?
6. What repartees did the Persian Ambassador make to Shah Jahan?
7. What kind of reproof did Aurangzeb give to his old teacher?
8. What was Bernier's opinion of Delhi and Agra?

SUBJECTS FOR ESSAYS

1. Contrast the conditions of Travel Now and in the Days of Aurangzeb.
2. After reading pages 30-33 write a description of some Modern City.
3. What do you think Aurangzeb would say about the System of Education in India to-day, if he were to come to life?

III

THE HOME-COMING

BY RABINDRANATH TAGORE

In all the history of literature there is no parallel case to that of Dr. Rabindranath Tagore, who first made a name for himself as a Bengali poet, and then, by accident as it were, burst upon the world at its time of greatest trouble, with a body of simple poetry of the heart, claiming no excellence of language, adopting no form even, save that of the old English translation of the psalms of King David, and yet so deep in consolation, in reminders of the loveliness of the life men were destroying so ruthlessly.

Nearly twenty years ago, Dr. Tagore told me in Japan how he had been detained in hospital in Bombay and had amused himself by making prose paraphrases of some of his early Bengali lyrics. On arrival in England he showed these to our mutual friend, now Sir William Rothenstein, and the result was the publication of *Gitanjuli* and the winning of the prize founded by Alfred Nobel for pre-eminence in Literature. A greater result was that his message of the joy to be found in the simplest things of home was borne by translation into every civilized people on earth, and for years now Dr. Tagore has been the Poet Laureate of the world.

> Thou art the last
> Of all the prophets, with a vast
> On-surging nation at thy feet,
> Whose frontiers widen round thy seat.

Dr. Tagore is equally remarkable as a critic of the highest kind, writing a rich and scholarly prose which has rarely been equalled by anyone who has written it as a foreign language. There is a great treat in store for any one who slowly passes from such stories as the following to the more difficult English of *Sadhana* and such lectures as the one he delivered at Dacca on the *Meaning of Art*.

PHATIK CHAKRAVARTI was the ringleader among the boys of the village. One day a plan for new mischief entered his head. There was a heavy log lying on the mud-flat of the river, waiting to be shaped into a mast for a boat. His plan was that they should all work together to shift the log by main force from its place and roll it away. The owner of the log would be angry and surprised, while they would all enjoy the fun. Every one supported the proposal, and it was carried unanimously.

But just as the fun was about to begin, Makhan, Phatik's younger brother, sauntered up without a word and sat down on the log in front of them all. The boys were puzzled for a moment. One of them pushed him rather timidly, and told him to get up; but he remained quite unconcerned. He appeared like a young philosopher meditating on the futility of games. Phatik was furious. Makhan', he cried, 'if you don't get up this minute, I'll thrash you?'

Makhan only moved to a more comfortable position. Now, if Phatik was to keep his regal dignity before the public, it was clear that he must carry out his threat. But his courage failed him at the crisis. His fertile brain, however, rapidly seized upon a new manœuvre which would discomfit his brother and afford his followers added amusement. He gave the word of command to roll the log and Makhan over together. Makhan heard the order and made it a point of honour to stick on. But like those who attempt earthly fame in other matters, he overlooked the fact that there was peril in it.

The boys began to heave at the log with all their might, calling out: 'One, two, three, go!' At the word 'go' the log went; and with it went Makhan's philosophy, glory and all.

The other boys shouted themselves hoarse with delight.

But Phatik was a little frightened. He knew what was coming. And he was not mistaken, for Makhan rose from Mother Earth blind as Fate and screaming like the Furies. He rushed at Phatik, scratched his face, beat him and kicked him, and then went crying home. The first act of the drama was over.

Phatik wiped his face, and sitting down on the edge of a sunken barge by the river-bank, began to nibble a piece of grass. A boat came up to the landing and a middle-aged man, with grey hair and dark moustache, stepped on shore. He saw the boy sitting there doing nothing and asked him where the Chakravartis lived. Phatik went on nibbling the grass and said: 'Over there,' but it was quite impossible to tell where he pointed. The stranger asked him again. He swung his legs to and fro on the side of the barge and said: 'Go and find out,' and continued to nibble the grass.

But, at that moment, a servant came down from the house and told Phatik that his mother wanted him. Phatik refused to move. But on this occasion the servant was the master. He roughly took Phatik up and carried him, kicking and struggling in powerless rage.

When Phatik entered the house, his mother saw him, and called out angrily: 'So you have been hitting Makhan again?'

Phatik answered indignantly: 'No. I haven't! Who told you that I had?'

His mother shouted: 'Don't tell lies! You have.'

Phatik said sullenly: 'I tell you, I haven't. You ask Makhan!' But Makhan thought it best to stick to his previous statement. He said: 'Yes, Mother, Phatik did hit me.'

Phatik's patience was already exhausted. He could not bear this injustice. He rushed at Makhan and rained on him a shower of blows: 'Take that,' he cried, 'and that, and that, for telling lies.'

His mother took Makhan's side in a moment, and pulled Phatik away, returning his blows with equal vigour. When Phatik pushed her aside, she shouted out: 'What! you little villain! Would you hit your own mother?'

It was just at this critical moment that the grey-haired stranger arrived. He asked what had occurred. Phatik looked sheepish and ashamed.

But when his mother stepped back and looked at the stranger, her anger was changed to surprise. For she recognised her brother and cried: 'Why, Dada! Where have you come from?'

As she said these words, she bowed to the ground and touched his feet. Her brother Bishamber had gone away soon after she had married, and had started business in Bombay. She herself had lost her husband while he was there. Bishamber had now come back to Calcutta, and had at once made enquiries concerning his sister. As soon as he found out where she was, he had hastened to see her.

The next few days were full of rejoicing. The brother asked how the two boys were being brought up. He was told by his sister that Phatik was a perpetual nuisance. He was lazy, disobedient, and wild. But Makhan was as good as gold, as quiet as a lamb, and very fond of reading. Bishamber kindly offered to take Phatik off his sister's hands and educate him with his own children in Calcutta. The widowed mother readily agreed. When his uncle asked Phatik if he would like to go to Calcutta with him, his joy knew no bounds and he said: 'Oh, yes, uncle!' in a way that made it quite clear that he meant it.

It was an immense relief to the mother to get rid of Phatik. She had a prejudice against the boy, and no love was lost between the two brothers. She was in daily fear that he would some day either drown Makhan in the river, or break his head in fight, or urge him on into some danger. At the same time she was a little distressed to see Phatik's extreme eagerness to leave his home.

Phatik, as soon as all was settled, kept asking his uncle every minute when they were to start. He was on pins all day long with excitement and lay awake most of the night. He bequeathed to Makhan, for good, his fishing-rod, his big kite, and his marbles. Indeed, at this time of departure, his generosity towards Makhan was unbounded.

When they reached Calcutta, Phatik met his aunt for the first time. She was by no means pleased with this unnecessary addition to her family. She found her own three boys quite enough to manage without taking any one else. And to bring a village lad of fourteen into their midst was terribly upsetting. Bishamber should really have thought twice before committing such an indiscretion.

In this world there is no worse nuisance than a boy at the age of fourteen. He is neither ornamental nor useful. It is impossible to shower affection on him as on a smaller boy; and he is always getting in the way. If he talks with a childish lisp he is called a baby, and if in a grown-up way he is called impertinent. In fact, talk of any kind from him is resented. Then he is at the unattractive, growing age. He grows out of his clothes with indecent haste; his voice grows hoarse and breaks and quavers; his face grows suddenly angular and unsightly. He becomes painfully self-conscious,. and when he talks with elderly people he is either unduly forward, or else so unduly shy that he appears ashamed of his own existence.

Yet, it is at this age that, in his heart of hearts, a young lad most craves recognition and love; and he becomes the devoted slave of any one who shows him consideration. But none dare openly love him, for that would be regarded as undue indulgence and therefore bad for the boy. So, what with scolding and chiding, he becomes very much like a stray dog that has lost its master.

His own home is the only Paradise that a boy of fourteen can know. To live in a strange house with strange people is little short of torture; while it is the height of bliss to receive the kind looks of women and never to suffer their slights.

It was anguish to Phatik to be an unwelcome guest in his aunt's house, constantly despised and slighted by this elderly woman. If she ever asked him to do anything for her, he would be so overjoyed that his joy would seem exaggerated; and then she would tell him not to be so stupid, but to get on with his lessons.

This constant neglect gave Phatik a feeling of almost physical oppression. He wanted to go out into the open country and fill his lungs with fresh air. But there was no open country to go to. Surrounded on all sides by Calcutta houses and walls, he would dream night after night of his village home and long to be back there.

He remembered the glorious meadow where he used to fly his kite all day long; the broad river-banks where he would wander the livelong day singing and shouting for joy; the narrow brook where he could dive and swim whenever he liked. He thought of the band of boy companions over whom he was despot; and, above all, thoughts of even that tyrant mother of his, who had such a prejudice against him, filled his mind day and night. A kind of physical love like that of animals, a longing to be in the presence of the loved one, an inexpressible wistfulness during absence, a silent cry of the inmost heart for the mother, like the lowing calf in the twilight,—this love, which was almost an animal instinct, stirred the heart of this shy, nervous, thin, uncouth and ugly boy. No one could understand it, but it preyed upon his mind continually.

There was no more backward boy in the whole school than Phatik. He gaped and remained silent when the teacher asked him a question, and like an overladen ass patiently suffered the many thrashings that were meted out to him. When other boys were out at play, he stood wistfully by the window and gazed at the roofs of the distant houses. And if by chance he espied children playing on the open terrace of a roof, his heart would ache with longing.

One day he summoned up all his courage and asked his uncle: 'Uncle, when can I go home?'

His uncle answered: 'Wait till the holidays come.'

But the holidays would not come till October and there was still a long time to wait.

One day Phatik lost his lesson book. Even with the help of books he had found it very difficult to prepare his lesson. But now it became impossible. Day after day the teacher caned him unmercifully. He became so miserable that even his cousins were ashamed to own him. They began to jeer and insult him more than even the other boys did. At last he went to his aunt and told her that he had lost his book.

With an expression of the greatest contempt she burst out: 'You great, clumsy, country lout! How can I afford to buy you new books five times a month, when I have my own family to look after?'

That night, on his way back from school, Phatik had a bad headache and a shivering-fit. He felt that he was going to have an attack of malaria. His one great fear was that he might be a nuisance to his aunt.

The next morning Phatik was nowhere to be seen. Search in the neighbourhood proved futile. The rain had been pouring in torrents all night, and those who went out to look for the boy were drenched to the skin. At last Bishamber asked the police to help him.

At nightfall a police van stopped at the door of the house. It was still raining and the streets were flooded. Two constables carried Phatik out in their arms and placed him before Bishamber. He was wet through from head to foot, covered with mud, while his face and eyes were flushed with fever and his limbs were trembling. Bishamber carried him in his arms and took him inside the house. When his wife saw him she exclaimed: 'What a heap of trouble this boy has given us! Hadn't you better send him home?'

Phatik heard her words and sobbed aloud: 'Uncle, I was just going home; but they dragged me back again.'

The fever rapidly increased, and throughout the night

the boy was delirious. Bishamber brought in a doctor. Phatik opened his eyes, and looking up to the ceiling said vacantly : 'Uncle, have the holidays come yet ?'

Bishamber wiped the tears from his eyes and took Phatik's thin burning hands in his own and sat by his side through the night. Again the boy began to mutter, till at last his voice rose to a shriek: 'Mother!' he cried, 'don't beat me like that . . . Mother! I am telling the truth!'

The next day Phatik for a short time became conscious. His eyes wandered round the room, as if he expected some one to come. At last, with an air of disappointment, his head sank back on the pillow. With a deep sigh he turned his face to the wall.

Bishamber read his thoughts, and bending down his head whispered: 'Phatik, I have sent for your mother.'

The day dragged on. The doctor said in a troubled voice that the boy's condition was very critical.

Phatik began to cry out: 'By the mark—three fathoms. By the mark—four fathoms. By the mark———.' Many times had he heard the sailors on the river-steamers calling out the mark on the leadline. Now he was himself plumbing an unfathomable sea.

Later in the day Phatik's mother burst into the room like a whirlwind, and rocking herself to and fro from side to side began to moan and cry.

Bishamber tried to calm her, but she flung herself on the bed, and cried: 'Phatik, my darling, my darling.'

Phatik stopped his restless movements for a moment. His hands ceased beating up and down. He said: 'Eh'?

The mother cried again: 'Phatik, my darling, my darling.'

Very slowly Phatik's eyess wandered, but he could no

longer see the people round his bed. At last he murmured: 'Mother, the holidays have come.'

NOTES

Sauntered: walked leisurely.
Futility: uselessness.
Regal: royal, kingly.
P. 36, l. 20. Failed him when most needed.
Manoeuvre: plan, device.
Discomfit: defeat his intentions, thwart.
Barge: a heavy flat-bottomed river-boat.
Sheepish: foolish.
Nuisance: something annoying. *Nuisance* is a very common word in England, for anything which causes us trouble. 'What a nuisance!' we say, and: 'That child is a terrible nuisance.'
On pins: anxiously expecting something. We generally say: On pins and needles.
Despot: the only master, tyrant.
Uncouth: awkward, clumsy.
Lout: fellow without any manners.
Flushed: red.
Delirious: out of his senses.
Leadline: line with a lump of lead attached for measuring the depth of water. This operation is called *sounding* or *plumbing*. So the passage means that he was passing through deep waters, as we say, that is, he was dying.

QUESTIONS

1. Tell in a few words the episode of Makhan on the log.
2. How did Phatik treat the man from the boat?
3. What do you think of his rudeness to his mother?
4. What happened when the man from the boat reached the house where the brothers lived?
5. What does Dr. Tagore say of boys of fourteen?
6. What were the feelings of Phatik on reaching his uncle's home?
7. What were the things he missed most?
8. Why did Phatik run away?
9. Tell the story of Phatik's last hours of life.
10. What do you feel is the moral of this sad story?

SUBJECTS FOR ESSAYS

1. A Scene from Home Life.
2. Boys at Mischief.
3. A Mother's Love.

IV

JAPAN

By Sir Syed Ross Masood

Sir Syed Ross Masood, one of the outstanding personalities of India in culture, charm and varied ability, is a son of the famous jurist Syed Mahmood, of whom it has been said that 'nobody ever approached him with a petition who did not get more than he wanted. He was a very jovial man, whose heart was quite as large and as tender as his intellect was acute and bright. You could not have a better and a truer friend.' And of no one are these words more true than of his distinguished son, till lately the eminent Vice-Chancellor of the University at Aligarh which his great and noble grand-father, Sir Syed Ahmed Khan founded in 1875.

Sir Ross Masood, after a career at Cambridge and practice as a barrister for a time, devoted his life to the education of his people. For a number of years he acted as Director of Public Instruction to H.E.H. the Nizam's Government, and in Hyderabad he is gratefully remembered for the stimulus he gave to all grades of education, working in close collaboration with his friend Sir Akbar Hydari. Together they entirely reorganised the Educational system of this large country and their work culminated in the successful establishment of the Osmania University, the first university in India to adopt the language of State as the medium of instruction.

It was as a result of his first visit to Japan in 1922 that Sir Ross Masood published his book on the Educational System of that country, from which the following passage is taken.

[*Note.* In India Japan is often wrongly pronounced as Jāpan. It should be Japán.]

Japan, as will be evident from its formation on the map of the world, has been most aptly likened to the emerged crests of submarine mountains. The country, consisting as it does of more than three thousand islands, is in reality an archipelago, and is said to be mainly the product of volcanic forces, which are even now by no means insignificant. It possesses about two hundred volcanoes, of which fifty continue more or less in a state of eruption.

The dire result of the presence of so many volcanoes can be traced in the sad loss of life that occupies so large a place in the ancient annals of the country; and even in modern days, there took place, between the years 1884 and 1905, no fewer than 30,680 earthquakes, which yield the very high average of about 4 shocks a day. Indeed, it was soon after my arrival in the country, that I had the misfortune to witness the biggest earthquake shock that had occurred within the previous 20 years; and I can never forget the feeling of utter helplessness that came over me at the sight of houses tumbling down and human beings getting crushed to death.[1]

But these volcanoes, while causing periodic destruction, have also enriched Japan in more ways than one. They have given to her so many sulphur and mineral springs, of different medicinal values, that it is quite possible that in the near future she will become perhaps the most important country in the world for water-cure treatment. Moreover, the volcanic deposits enrich the already excellent soil of the country, and thus help to increase the fertility of the whole land, on which, indeed, the greater part of the nation is almost entirely dependent for its subsistence.

In addition to the above, numerous metals and minerals are also found in the country—gold, silver, copper, lead, tin, iron, petroleum and coal. So extensive, indeed, are the deposits of the last-named mineral that almost all the foreign ships that pass Japan use her ports for coaling purposes, and this forms a big source of revenue for the people. The seas, too, that surround Japan offer to the nation an inexhaustible supply of food, for, they are full of a large variety of the choicest edible fish, which, with boiled rice, forms the chief diet of the inhabitants.

[1] This passage was written a year before the Great Earthquake of 1923.

In area Japan proper is a little over 142,000 square miles, and, according to the last census, taken at midnight on the 10th October 1920, has a population of 55,961,140. The total population for the whole Empire, including Korea, Formosa, Saghalien Islands, etc., is 77,005,510.[1] Thus, for purposes of comparison, the area of Japan proper may be said to be considerably less than twice that of the Hyderabad Dominions, and its population more than five times as great.

My study of the history of Japan disclosed to me certain very striking similarities between that country and England. Her position on the map of Asia has many features in common with that of England on the map of Europe. Then again, as the climate of England is warmed by the flow of the Gulf Stream, so is that of Japan modified by the flow of the *Kuroshiwo* or Black Stream, which rises near the Equator and is produced by the Pacific Trade Winds. As England was threatened by the great Spanish Armada in the days of Queen Elizabeth in the year 1588, so was Japan by the huge Mongol Fleet sent by Kublai Khan towards the end of the 13th century (1281) with the object of annexing it to his dominions. The Spanish Armada was driven away by a storm, and in the same way the Mongol Fleet was blown away from the shores of Japan with great loss of life. The boats of the enemies of Japan were 'impaled on the rocks, dashed against the cliffs, or tossed on land like corks from the spray'. The English commemorated their deliverance from their enemy by having a coin struck with the words: 'God breathed and

[1] In October 1925 these numbers had increased to 59,736,822 and 83,456,929

they were scattered', and the Japanese said that their gods and their heaven prevailed over the gods and the heaven of the enemy.

Finally, as the partial seclusion of England from the general stream of Continental life tended to weld its different elements into one nation, so did that of Japan; and as regrads the intellectual development of the race, what Norman France did to civilize Saxon England, Korea did to Japan; for, it was from China, through Korea, that Japan received her first civilisation.

From the point of view of ethnology also, the Japanese nation of to-day is the result of the intermingling of as many different elements as have produced the English nation. The latter is the product of the intermingling of Celts, Saxons, Angles, Jutes, Danes, and Normans; and in the Japanese nation, as we find it today, have been incorporated the racial types of China, Malay Archipelago, Korea, Tartary, Mongolia and, to some extent, India.

All these common features have produced in the Japanese people traits similar to those found in the English people; and in the course of my stay amongst them, I was again and again struck with these similarities. The same insular reserve is to be found amongst the Japanese as amongst the English, and in seamanship they have shown the same hardihood, coolheadedness, and valour, which have made England the greatest naval power of the modern world.

But there are two features in their history, which are not found in that of any other country: the first is that the Emperors of the present family have continued to rule since the legendary era: and the second that, though several attempts were made to conquer Japan, the invaders were in every case defeated and driven away.

Perhaps the most remarkable characteristic of the Japanese race is their intense patriotism and loyalty to their country; and it would be no exaggeration to say that these two sentiments form the foundation on which the entire fabric of modernized Japan has been reared. On questioning boys belonging to different educational institutions and of different ages, as to what was their greatest ambition in life, I invariably received the answer: 'Sir, we want an opportunity to die for the glory of our country and of our Emperor.' This answer was always given with a genuineness which seemed to me most impressive.

The Japanese consider themselves as belonging to one family, and their Emperor as its head or patriarch; and what is truly remarkable is that this intimate relation has continued from the first foundation of the Empire down to the present day.

To understand the subsequent developments in the history of Japan, it should be fully realized that they do not regard their Emperor merely as a reigning Sovereign, but believe him to be a living God. So intense indeed is the veneration in which the Emperor is held, that, unlike the nations of Europe, the Japanese have never deemed it right to have the head of their ruler either on their postage stamps or on their coins. The natural wear and tear to which these are subjected, would, in their eyes, be a sacrilege if they were allowed to bear the features of the Emperor. We find that there was, as late as 1868, a law about the public sale and display of the portrait of the Emperor. All such pictures were forbidden, and any one found guilty of allowing them to remain exposed to the public gaze was at once executed. Even today, when the sale of the photographs of the Emperor is encouraged the idea of letting his face remain unprotected is distasteful to the people. They, invariably, even in their shops, keep such portraits either wrapped in cloth or covered with paper.

No incident that I know can show better the divine honour paid to the Emperor, than the one that occurred in a school not long ago. Fire had broken out, and a pupil rushed through the flames into the principal's room, where, as is the case in all the schools in Japan, a portrait of the Emperor was kept. Seeing that he could no longer carry it out in safety, the boy at once took the picture out of the frame, cut open his abdomen, and thrusting it into his body, tried to rush out, but was scorched to death by the flames that had now burst forth with still greater fury. The people recovered the picture which, though crumpled, was found to be none the less unscathed.

Nor do the Japanese ever allow any one to see their Emperor from a position higher than his. The law today is that whenever the Emperor passes through a street, all blinds and curtains must be tightly drawn, and all the occupants must come down into the road. Even the unfortunate Europeans, who are naturally ignorant of this rule, cannot escape it. The police records are full of the cases of Englishmen and Americans, who, on hearing from their rooms in hotels a noise in the street, have opened the windows to see what was happening, and, being detected by the police, have been taken at once before a magistrate and charged with the offence of gazing at the emperor of Japan from an elevated position.

Quite recently, the mayor of a small country village, not knowing the real but only the assumed name of the Emperor, allowed a boy to be named Yoshihito, and registered him as such in the village book. When the fact was discovered, he was asked to resign. But so horrified was he at his mistake, that he at once committed suicide.

A recent European writer, Dr. McGovern, has thus described the respect which the whole nation shows to the late Emperor Meiji, during whose rule Japan adopted European civilization and rose to the position of an important world-power :—

'The Emperor whose grave is the most popular and visited by pilgrims is the late Meiji Tenno, whose magnificent mausoleum at Momoyama, near Kyoto, is one of the most impressive sights of the world. Here, under the great white artificial mountain, lie the remains of the venerated ruler. A shrine has been erected before it, and before it day after day hundreds, and on holidays thousands, of pilgrims go and pay their homage—homage, not, as we of the West know it, to a dead hero, but to the invisible and all-powerful shade ever mindful of the petitions offered him, capable and willing of fulfilling them, for it is the belief of the Japanese that at death the soul is not allocated either to heaven or hell, but remains as a ghost haunting either the tomb in which lies his body or the shrine that has been erected to him. . . . . . Therefore is it that the shades of former rulers are supposed to be still watching over the land that they governed and loved; still will their spirits take pleasure in the adulation of the subjects of their successors; and all questions of national import, the making of war or the signing of peace, are solemnly reported to them, and their blessings asked upon the undertaking.'

Though the Japanese are capable of taking a very serious view of life, yet, on the whole, their nature is a gay one. The average Japanese goes through life with a smile on his lips ; and the little worries that, in the case of us Indians, play such frightful havoc with our peace of mind, do not disturb him. He looks upon them as part of the day's work.

Nevertheless, numerous are the suicides committed every year by students, whom the intense labour to which they subject themselves, in their attempt to acquire as rapidly as possible the highest standards of Western knowledge, throws into a gloom of despair. Thousands are the cases where the Japanese students, in order to be able to pay their college fees, have to work, during some portion of the day or night, as labourers. But so highly is self-respect valued by the entire nation, that begging for favours, specially for monetary help, so common in our country, is almost unknown.

I knew a student in one of the universities at Tokyo, who was compelled, in order to meet the expenses of his education, to live on a field six miles away as its care-taker. He used to cook his own food in the morning at dawn, tramp out to the University, since he could not afford to go in any conveyance, and live practically on one meal a day. When I came to know the extraordinary refinement of his character, and really marvellous power of judgment, I offered to give him some monetary help. Never will I forget the look of intense pain that came over his face, when, in a most dignified but polite manner, he told me that, since in his veins flowed the blood of the warriors of old Japan, it was his duty to face, unaided, and in as manly a manner as possible, all the obstacles that came in his way. It was then that I realized, for the first time, the manliness and earnestness that lie hid behind the smiling face and the polite manners of the inhabitants of Japan.

There also come to my mind the heroic suicides of several Japanese widows, during the Russo-Japanese War, so as to make it possible for their only sons to go to fight for their country, since the only sons of widows were not allowed by the law of the land to enlist themselves as soldiers.

I feel, and feel strongly, that a nation possessing the tremendous patriotism of the Japanese can never suffer the moral and political degradation, through which the greater part of the world has passed, of allowing itself to be conquered by people of a foreign race.

The training given in Old Japan to the Samurai, who, like the Kshatrias of ancient India, monopolized the military profession, has tended to create a type of man surely unique in the 20th century. It, however, still remains to be seen whether the present-day close connection with the commercial forces of the West will tend to weaken the native heroism and chivalry of the race or not. Personally, I feel that the heroic deeds of their ancestors—and there are thousands of them in the annals of Old Japan—will ever remain a perpetual source of inspiration to the Japanese; and, whatever be the influences with which they come into contact, the sentiments that for centuries past have become part of the very soul of the nation will never be uprooted and destroyed.

The first thing that used to be taught to the Samurai was to suppress completely all display of emotion. He was taught to face pain, pleasure, and peril without showing the slightest sign of trouble; and this still forms the chief characteristic of the Japanese soldier.

What deed of bravery can be higher than that evidenced in the Russo-Japanese War before the gates of Port Arthur? The episode is thus described by an Englishman: 'When volunteers were asked to undertake the blocking of Port Arthur, over two thousand offered themselves for the dangerous task, and some of the applications were written with the blood of the men who sent them in. Seventy-seven officers and men were selected, and the farewell ceremonies which were held were of a striking and touching nature. On board the battleship *Asama*, Captain Yashiro took a large silver cup presented to him by His Imperial Highness the Crown Prince, and filling it with water (it being an old Japanese custom to drink water on the occasion of permanent parting between near relatives), thus addressed the volunteers: "In sending you now on the duty of blocking the harbour entrance of Port Arthur, which affords you one chance out of thousands to return alive, I feel as if I were sending my beloved sons. But if I had one hundred sons, I would send them all on such a bold adventure as this, and had I only one son I should wish to do the same with him. In performing your duty, if you happen to lose your left hand, work with your right; if you lose both hands, work with both feet; if you lose both feet, work with your head, and faithfully carry out the orders of your commander. I send you to the place of death, and I have no doubt that you are quite ready to die. However, I do not mean to advise you to despise your life nor to run needless risks in trying to establish a great name. What I ask you all is to perform your duty regardless of your life. The cup of water I give you now is not meant to give you encouragement but to appoint you representatives of the bravery of the *Asama*. A great shame it would be if our men needed Dutch courage to go to the place of death! I look forward to a joyous day when I see you again coming back with success. Submit your life to the will of Heaven and calmly perform your hard duty." Among the volunteers was Commander Hirose. Before the first attempt on Port Arthur he wrote home: "How can I refuse to die as a patriotic sacrifice for my country? It will be a glorious death to go down with the ship at the entrance of Port Arthur." Before the second attempt, in which he perished, he wrote: "Knowing that the souls of the brave return seven times to this world to serve their country, I sacrifice with confidence this life, and expecting now to achieve final success I will go on board the ship cheerfully." '

This heroism is the outcome of the rule which every one, from the highest to the lowest, is taught to obey, that 'it is the imperative duty of man in his capacity of a subject, to sacrifice his private interests to the public good. Selfishness forbids co-operation, and without co-operation there cannot be any great achievement.'

Samurai men, women, and children were, in Old Japan, taught the use of the sword. It was laid down in their code of honour that a Samurai should never surrender himself in battle to his enemy. Thus, we find, in the history of Japan, thousands of instances of soldiers and their commanders committing *harakiri* (or suicide) on the field of battle when defeated, rather than allow themselves to become captives. Indeed, to the institution of *harakiri* legal sanction was accorded before the dawn of the modern era in Japan; and even today the courage to take one's own life ranks very high in the estimate of the nation, and there is no stigma attached to it.

Formerly, criminals of the Samurai class were allowed by the Government, when found guilty, to destroy themselves instead of being handed over to the public executioner; and this concession was deemed a great boon. The time and place used to be officially notified to the condemned, and officials had orders to witness the ceremony. The men committed suicide in a sitting posture by disembowelling themselves, without letting the slightest look of agony appear on their faces, and the women did it by cutting their throats.

It is still a belief in Japan that there are only two ways in which an insult can be wiped out: the first is by killing him who insults, and the second, by killing oneself; for existence without having washed away an insult is deemed unworthy. Thus foreigners, who visit Japan, have to be very careful in dealing with the people of the country whatever be the class of society to which they belong.

An Indian friend of mine, who has settled down in Yokohama as a merchant, described to me very vividly how, on one occasion, he had placed himself quite unknowingly in a horrible position. Being in a hurry, he had thrown down a coin to the cooly who was accompanying him. Great was his horror when he saw the face of the man grow red with anger, and heard him demand in a fierce way why the crest of the Emperor, which was embossed on the coin, had been insulted by being thrown on the ground. Luckily for my friend, any further unpleasantness was stopped by the timely arrival of a Japanese acquaintance, who, taking in the situation at a glance, at once lifted the coin from the pavement, and handed it to the cooly in a respectful manner, and at the same time warned my friend not to make such a mistake again.

So high indeed is the regard paid by the Japanese to the self-respect of other human beings, that it always amazed me to see parents addressing their little children in exactly the same polite manner in which they addressed people of their own position in life.

Thus, though self-respect, love for their country, and intense loyalty for their Emperor are produced by all the means possible, yet, I cannot help feeling that this has resulted in making the Japanese perhaps the most sensitive nation in the world, and this so much so, that the average foreigner finds it most difficult to be on that footing of intimacy with them which is so common both amongst us and amongst the Europeans. This extreme sensitiveness, together with commercial rivalry, are I find to a large extent responsible for the dislike with which the inhabitants of Japan are beginning to be regarded by other nations.

To show how even the poorest classes in Japan regard questions of national honour, it will suffice to quote the personal experience of an English Bishop which has been very kindly communicated to me by a friend. The Bishop had made a journey in Japan on which all his luggage had been lost, though he had taken every precaution to have it duly directed and registered. He was annoyed when he reached Tokyo, to find that the luggage had been put out somewhere else. The railway officials only assured him that they would send it on by a handcart, if he would leave the money for it, as soon as it reached the station.

The Bishop replied: 'If this had happened in England, the luggage would have been sent on by the Company free of charge.' After this, he saw three or four railway-men consult together, and one of them came forward and said that his luggage would reach him free of charge. The Bishop had not been long in Japan at the time, and did not know that the railways were entirely in the hands of Government, and that the officials were very poorly paid. But he did enquire into the matter, and found that the railway-men were so hurt at the idea of England surpassing Japan in anything, that they agreed at once to club together and pay out of their poor salaries the expense of forwarding the luggage to the Bishop.

As regards the women of Japan, I hold a very high opinion. I look upon them as perhaps the most perfect product of culture. In artistic feeling and understanding I believe them to be at least a hundred years ahead of the women of France, whom Europe has ever regarded as the most artistic in that part of the world. Never having been subjected to the seclusion of the kind in which our women have lived for centuries, they possess that freedom of thought and movement which is by no means common in India. They are physically strong without being brutal, extremely modest without being dependent, and entirely unselfish in the despatch of their daily duties. The woman of Japan has proved herself 'patient in the hour of suffering; strong in time of affliction; a faithful wife; a loving mother; a good daughter; and capable, as history shows, of heroism rivalling that of the stronger sex.' Indeed, the seriousness with which she regards her duties as a human being will be fully realised when I state that divorces on account of a wife's unfaithfulness are almost wholly unknown in Japan. A great authority has well summed up the chief characteristics of the whole nation in the sentence: 'Frugality, industry and patience characterize all the bread-winners; courage and burning patriotism are attributes of the whole nation.'

The code of Samurai honour has impressed itself as deeply on the psychology and the daily behaviour of the women of Japan as on that of its men. Since one of the chief rules of Japanese politeness is to avoid placing on a stranger the weight of one's own troubles, a Japanese mother, coming out from the room, where she has been giving way to utmost grief, will quite calmly describe to a stranger the death of her only child. It is owing to their inability to understand such heroic suppression of emotions that foreigners often make the mistake of calling the Japanese insincere.

I find, that though today in Japan, as indeed in other parts of the world, the field of battle has been exchanged for the field of commerce, yet, there, unlike elsewhere, the forces that produced the perfect Samurai continue quite strong, especially in human relations; the only thing that has changed is the way those forces are shown. As in the days of old, so to-day, often do faithful servants try, by means of dying protest, to turn their masters from following a course injurious to their reputation and fortune.

As in the schools of Old Japan the sons of Samurai were taught military arts and afterwards made to travel in the country, so I find that in the schools of Modern Japan physical education occupies a most important place in the course. Teachers and pupils set out on long tramps, carrying their own provisions with them, and get accustomed to the inclemency of the weather. If a proper test of physical fitness were to be held throughout the world, I am inclined to think that the Japanese, in spite of being an ancient race, would come out very high indeed.

As regards their history, they are today as intensely proud of it as ever before, and, unlike us, pay very great attention to the making and preserving of their national records.

The other facts that struck me as really remarkable in the history of the Japanese people are that with them, unlike elsewhere, the perfect Samurai had always to be both a soldier and a scholar; and religious bigotry was unknown till their first contact with Christian Europe towards the middle of the Sixteenth Century.

In personal cleanliness there is no nation today that comes up to the Japanese. Not to be clean is considered a great social crime by the rich and the poor alike; consequently, Japanese houses are the neatest and cleanest dwellings in the world.

NOTES

Archipelago: group of islands.
Subsistence: food. The Japanese largely *subsist* on rice and fish.
Edible: eatable.
Impaled: formerly people were impaled, as a form of execution. It was a horrible punishment by which a man was pierced with an upright stake and left thus to die.
Weld: welding is the uniting of pieces of metal, generally by extreme pressure. The meaning is that as the people of England and Japan were separated by the sea from other peoples, the English and the Japanese each became one nation with all its elements well united.
Ethnology: the study of races of people.
Incorporated: united in one body or nation. The Latin word *corpus* means a body; *corpse* is a dead body; *corps* (pron. core) a body of soldiers or diplomats. *Corporal punishment* means beating the body.
Traits: (pron. *trays* not *traits*). Distinct marks of character.

Insular reserve: *reserve* means self-restraint which makes a person seem cool, or without heartiness. *Insular* is the adjective of *island*. The English are an insular people. So *insular* has also come to mean *reserved*.

Hardihood: boldness. **Coolheadedness:** Self-control in danger.

Fabric: structure. **Patriarch:** venerable ruler.

Intense veneration: very strong reverence.

P. 49, l. 28. Money is much handled, and so coins become worn or defaced. The Japanese thought that it would be sacrilege, or a violation of sacred majesty, to print an Emperor's face on a coin.

Unscathed: undamaged. **Homage:** worship, reverence.

Adulation: flattery. **Monetary:** financial (adjective of *money*).

Blocking: by sinking the ships in which they were sailing.

Disembowelling themselves: Cutting themselves deeply across the stomach.

Sensitive: look up in the dictionary the difference between the four adjectives sensitive, sensible, sensual and sensuous.

Without being dependent: dependent upon others. That is they could act freely and do things of their own accord.

Inclemency: cold and stormy nature. *Clement* really means kind

QUESTIONS

1. What does the author say about volcanoes?
2. What points of comparison between Japan and England are noted?
3. What is said about the great ambition of Japanese schoolboys?
4. What are the things which have struck you most in the account of Japanese loyalty to the Emperor?
5. Tell the story of the poor student living on a field.
6. What does the author say about the Samurai?
7. Tell the story of the dedication of the men of the *Asama*.
8. What is the author's view of the results of Japanese self-respect?
9. What does the author think of the women of Japan?

SUBJECTS FOR ESSAYS

1. What Young India can learn from Japan.
2. The physical features of India contrasted with those of Japan.
3. On Self-Respect.
4. Japanese Loyalty.
5. On True Heroism.
6. National Characteristics of the Japanese.

V

GOKHALE THE MAN

BY SAROJINI NAIDU

The name of Mrs. Sarojini Naidu has two noble associations which have made her known throughout the English-speaking world,—her poetry and her patriotic enthusiasm and endeavour. To those who are privileged to enjoy her friendship, her personal charm of sympathy, brightness and humour invest these exalted pursuits with a meaning which the mere written words are not enough to convey. Her speeches must be heard from the delighted audience; her songs must be listened to with their gesture and the accompaniment of a musical voice. For Mrs. Naidu is above all a singer, a lyrical personality, to which she adds a very remarkable power of choosing and arranging words, almost as a jeweller inlays his gold with gems. And yet this does not imply that she uses words merely as decoration. Nobody can be more to the point, and sharply, memorably so, than Mrs. Naidu. Her English reveals a very remarkable blend of sense and song, as might be naturally expected from the daughter of such a brilliant and lovable father as Dr. Aghoranath, of whom Mrs. Naidu has written:

> My ancestors for thousands of years have been lovers of the forests and mountain caves, great dreamers, great scholars, great ascetics. My father is a dreamer himself, a great dreamer, a great man whose life has been a magnificent failure. I suppose in the whole of India there are few men whose learning is greater than his, and I don't think there are many men more beloved. He has a great white beard and the profile of Homer and a laugh that brings the roof down. He has wasted all his money on two great objects: to help others and on alchemy. He holds huge courts every day in his garden of all the learned men of all religions—Rajas and beggars and saints and downright villains, all delightfully mixed up, and all treated as one. And then, his alchemy! Oh dear, night and day the experiments are going on, and every man who brings a new prescription is welcome as a brother! But this alchemy is, you know, only the material counterpart of a poet's craving for Beauty, the eternal Beauty. 'The makers of gold and the makers of verse,' they are twin creators that sway the world's secret desire for mystery; and what in my father is the genius of curiosity—

> the very essence of all scientific genius—in me is the desire for beauty. Do you remember Pater's phrase about Leonardo da Vinci, 'Curiosity and the desire of beauty'?

Mrs. Naidu's poetry is more popular in India than that of any other Indian poet writing in metrical English, and many people prefer it to the metric prose of Dr. Tagore's well-known books. The bulk of her prose is patriotic or political in origin and purport. The following tribute to Mr. Gokhale reveals her power in another direction.

I

A LOVELY COMRADESHIP

My personal association with Mr. Gokhale commenced, as it ended, with a written message. It had fallen to me to propose the resolution on the education of women at the Calcutta Sessions of the All-India Social Conference of 1906; and, something in my speech moved him sufficiently to pass me these hurried and cordial sentences which, unworthy as I know myself of such generous appreciation, I venture to transcribe, since they struck the keynote of all our future intercourse. 'May I take the liberty', he wrote, 'to offer you my most respectful and enthusiastic congratulations? Your speech was more than an intellectual treat of the highest order. It was a perfect piece of art. We all felt for the moment to be lifted to a higher plane.'

An acquaintance begun on such a happy note of sympathy, grew and ripened at the last into a close and lovely comradeship which I counted among the crowning honours of my life. And, though it was not without its painful moments of brief and bitter parting, our friendship was always radiant both with the joy of spiritual refreshment and the inspiring challenge of intellectual discussion and difference of opinion. Above all, there was the ever-deepening bond of our common love for the motherland;

and, for a short space, there was also the added tie of a tender dependence, infinitely touching and childlike, on such comfort and companionship as I, with my own broken health, could render him through long weeks of suffering and distress in a foreign land.

Between 1907 and 1911, it was my good fortune to meet him several times, chiefly during my flying visits to Bombay, but also on different occasions, in Madras, Poona and Delhi. After each meeting I would always carry away the memory of some stirring words of exhortation to yield my life to the service of India. And, even in the midst of the crowded activities of those epoch-making years, he found leisure to send me now and then a warm message of approval or encouragement, when any poem or speech or action of mine chanced to please him, or the frequent rumours of my failing health caused him anxiety or alarm.

But it was not till the beginning of 1912, when I spent a few weeks in Calcutta with my father, that any real intimacy was established between us. 'Hitherto I have always caught you on the wing,' he said, 'now I will cage you long enough to grasp your true spirit.' It was in the course of the long and delightful conversations of this period that I began to comprehend the real and many-sided greatness of the man, and to marvel by what stern and fruitful process he was able to unite the complex and often opposing qualities of his personality into so supreme an achievement of single-hearted patriotism. It was to me a valuable lesson in human psychology to study the secret of this rich and puzzling nature. There was the outer man as the world knew and esteemed him, with his precise and brilliant and subtle intellect, his unrivalled gifts of political analysis and synthesis, his flawless and relentless mastery and use of the consummate logic of facts and figures, his courteous but inexorable candour in opposition, his patient dignity and courage in honourable compromise, the breadth and restraint, the vigour and veracity of his far-reaching statesmanship, the lofty simplicities and sacrifices of his daily life. And, breaking through the veils of his many self-repressions, was the inner man that revealed himself to me, in all his intense and urgent need for human kinship and affection, in all the tumult and longing, the agony of doubt and ecstasy of faith of the born idealist perpetually seeking some unchanging reality in a world full of shifting disillusion and despair. In him, I felt that both the practical, strenuous worker and the mystic dreamer of dreams were harmonised by the agelong discipline of his Brahminical ancestry, which, centuries before, had evolved the spirit of the Bhagavad Gita and defined true Yoga as Wisdom in Action.

A conversation of that time stands out with special significance in the light of coming events. One morning, a little despondent and sick at heart about national affairs in general, he suddenly asked me: 'What is your outlook for India?' 'One of hope' I replied. 'What is your vision of the immediate future?' 'The Hindu-Muslim unity in less than five years', I told him with joyous conviction. 'Child', he said, with a note of yearning sadness in his voice, 'you are a poet, but you hope too much. It will not come in your lifetime or in mine. But keep your faith and work if you can.'

In March of the following year, I met him for a few minutes only, at a large party in Bombay given by Sir

Pherozshah Mehta for the members of the Royal Commission. I had recently brought out a new book of verses which just then, happily for me, was attracting some attention and applause. And Mr. Gokhale's short conversation with me was very characteristic of his attitude of distrust towards such things. 'Does the flame still burn brightly?' he questioned. 'Brighter than ever', I answered. But he shook his head doubtfully and a little sternly. 'I wonder', he murmured, 'I wonder how long it will withstand the storm of such excessive adulation and success.'

A week later, it was my unique privilege to attend and address the now historic sessions of the Muslim League which met in Lucknow on the 22nd March to adopt a new constitution which was the beginning of loyal co-operation with the sister community in all matters of national welfare and progress. The unanimous acclamation with which it was carried by both the older and younger schools of Mussalman politicians marked a new era and inaugurated a new standard in the history of modern Indian affairs. From Lucknow I travelled, almost without a break, direct to Poona, where I was due on the 25th and on the morning of the 26th, I walked across with the Honourable Mr. Paranjpye from Fergusson College to the Servants of India Society. I found the world-famous leader of the Indian National Congress weak and suffering from a relapse of his old illness, but busy scanning the journals that were full of comments and criticisms of the Muslim League and its new ideals. 'Ah', he cried, with outstretched hands when he saw me, 'have you come to tell me that your vision was true?' And he continued to question me over and over again with a breathless eagerness that seemed almost impatient of my words, about the real underlying *spirit* of the Conference.

After an hour or so I found him exhausted with the excitement of the happy news I had brought him from so far; but he insisted on my returning to complete my visit to him that afternoon. When I went back to the Servants of India Society in the evening, I found a strangely transformed Mr. Gokhale, brisk and smiling, a little pale, but without any trace of the morning's weariness and depression. 'What' I almost screamed, as he was preparing to lead the way upstairs. 'Surely you cannot mean to mount all those steps. You are too ill.' He laughed. 'You have put new hope into me', he said, 'I feel strong enough to face life and work again.'

Presently his sister and two charming daughters joined us for half an hour on the broad terrace with its peaceful view over sunset hills and valleys, and we talked of pleasant and passing things. This was my first and only glimpse and realization of the personal domestic side of this lonely and impersonal worker.

After their departure we sat quietly in the gathering twilight till his golden voice, stirred by some deep emotion, broke the silence with golden words of counsel and warning, so grand, so solemn, and so inspiring, that they have never ceased to thrill me. He spoke of the unequalled happiness and privilege of service for India. 'Stand here with me', he said, 'with the stars and hills for witness, and in their presence consecrate your life and your talent, your song and your speech, your thought and your dream to the Motherland. O Poet, see visions from the hill-tops and spread abroad the message of hope to the toilers in the valleys.'

As I took my leave of him, he said again, to this humble messenger of happy tidings, 'You have given me new hope, new faith, new courage. To-night I shall rest. I shall sleep with a heart at peace.'

II

IN ENGLAND

Two months later, early in June, after an absence of fifteen years, I found myself in London once more; and, among the many friends who greeted me on my arrival was the familiar figure of Mr. Gokhale in wholly unfamiliar European garments and—yes—actually an English top-hat. I stared at him for a moment. 'Where', I asked him, 'is your rebellious turban?' But I soon got accustomed to this new phase of my old friend, to a social Gokhale who attended parties and frequented theatres, played bridge and entertained ladies at dinner on the terrace of the National Liberal Club—a far cry from the terrace of the Servants of India Society.

In spite of his uncertain health, he was very busy throughout the summer with his work on the Royal Commission and his anxious pre-occupation with Indian affairs in South Africa, then threatening an acute crisis. But he would often come to see me where I was staying at the house of Sir Krishna Gupta. Mr. Gokhale had a great fancy for cherries, and I always took care to provide a liberal supply whenever he was expected. 'Every man has his price,' I would tease him, 'and yours is cherries.'

A few days later, on the 2nd August, he delivered a magnificent inaugural address at Caxton Hall in the presence of a large and enthusiastic audience of students, and set before them those sublime lessons of patriotism and self-sacrifice which he alone so signally, among the men of his generation, was competent to teach with authority and grace.

Shortly afterwards he left for India to wage his brave and glorious battle in the cause of his suffering compatriots in South Africa. And though now his health was finally ruined beyond all chance of recovery, it was with the rapture of victorious martyrdom that he wrote from his sick bed, about the end of December, to tell me how prompt and splendid had been the response of a truly united India to the call of her gallant heroes fighting for the eternal laws of right and justice in a far off land.

On his return to England in the Spring of 1914, his condition was so dangerous as to cause his friends and physicians the gravest concern; and at first he was confined entirely to bed. But with his ever-gracious kindness towards me, he paid me a visit on the very day he was permitted to leave his room, as I was then too ill to go and see him. 'Why should a song-bird like you have a broken wing?', he murmured a little sadly; and presently, he told me that he had just received his own death-warrant at the hands of his doctors. 'With the utmost care', he said, 'they think I might perhaps live for three years longer.' But, in his calm and thoughtful manner there was no sign of selfish rebellion or fear—only an infinite regret for his unfinished service to India.

Soon, however, I was well enough to accompany him

on the short motor drives that were his sole form of recreation; and on mild days, as we sat in the soft sunshine under the budding trees of Kensington Gardens he would talk to me with that sure instinct of his for choice and graphic phrases that lent his conversation so much distinction and charm. 'Give me a corner of your brain that I can call my own', he would say. And in that special corner that was his I treasure many memorable sayings. One day, a little wistfully he said: 'Do you know, I feel that an abiding sadness underlies all that unfailing brightness of yours? Is it because you have come so near death that its shadows still cling to you?' 'No', I answered, 'I have come so near life that its fires have burnt me.'

But, like a homing bird, his heart would always return with swift and certain flight to the one unchangeable passion of his life, his love for that India which to him was mistress and mother, goddess and child in one. He would speak of the struggles and disappointments of his early days, the triumphs and failures, the rewards and sacrifices of his later years, his vision of India and her final goal, her immediate value as an Imperial asset, her appointed place and purpose in the wider counsels and responsibilities of the Empire.

He spoke too of his work and his colleagues on the Royal Commission, the Viceregal Council and the National Congress; and though to the end he remained a better judge of human situations rather than of individuals, I was struck with the essential fairness of his estimates which seemed in one luminous phrase to reveal the true measure of a man. Of one he said that 'He can mould heroes out of common clay'; of another that 'He has fine sincerity a little marred by hasty judgement;' of yet another: 'He has true stuff in him and that freedom from all sectarian prejudice which will make him the best ambassador of Hindu-Muslim unity.' Of a fourth: 'He has made those sacrifices which entitle him to be heard.

Of the many pressing matters that occupied his mind at that time, there were four which to him were of absorbing interest. His scheme for compulsory education which, he felt, was the only solid basis on which to found any lasting national progress. The Hindu-Mussalman question which, he said, could be most fruitfully solved if the leaders of the sister communities would deal in a spirit of perfect unison with certain fundamental problems of equal and urgent importance to both. The high privilege and heavy responsibility of the young generation whose function it was to grapple with more immense and vital issues than his generation had been called upon to face. And of course, the future of the Servants of India Society, which was the actual embodiment of all his dreams and devotion for India.

These open-air conversations, however, came to a speedy end. He suddenly grew worse and was forbidden to leave his room or to receive visitors. But I was fortunate enough to be allowed to see him almost daily for a few hours till his departure for Vichy. In his whimsical way he would call me the best of all his prescriptions. To my usual query on crossing the threshold of his sickroom: 'Well; am I to be a stimulant or a sedative today?' his invariable reply was: 'Both'. And this one word most fitly summed up the need of his sinking heart and overburdened brain through these anxious and critical weeks.

The interval between his first and second visits to Vichy he spent in a quiet little cottage at Twickenham as the guest and neighbour of Mr. and Mrs. Ratan Tata, to whom the nation already owes so many debts of gratitude; and the monotony of the long hours of his temporary and interrupted convalescence was often brightened by the presence of friends whose visits to him were really pilgrimages, and solaced by the devoted attendance of Dr. Jivraj Mehta, who has since won such proud academic honours, and of whom Mr. Gokhale more than once said: 'He will go far, and be a leader of men.'

From Vichy he wrote: 'Here, in this intense mental solitude, I have come upon the bedrock truths of life and must learn to adjust myself to their demands.' The outbreak of war in August brought him back to England a little prematurely. But though his health had clearly improved, and he was better able to stand the strain of his arduous work on the Royal Commission, he seemed oppressed with a sharp and sudden sense of exile in the midst of an alien civilization and people, and to be haunted by a deep home-sickness which he himself could not explain, not merely for the wonted physical scenes and surroundings but for the spiritual texts and tongues of his ancestral land. His conversation during these days was steeped in allusion to the old Sanscrit writers whose mighty music was in his very blood.

The last occasion on which I saw him was on the 8th October, two days before I sailed for India. Something, maybe, of the autumnal sadness of fallen leaves and growing mists had passed into his mood; or, maybe, he felt the foreshadowing of the wings of Death. But as he bade me farewell, he said: 'I do not think we shall meet again. If you live, remember your life is dedicated to the service of the Country. My work is done.'

Early in December, shortly after his arrival from Europe, he wrote to complain of the 'scurvy trick' fate had played him in a renewal of his old trouble; but succeeding letters reported returning strength and ability to work again. In the last letter, written the day before his fatal illness, he spoke of his health being now stationary and of his coming visit to Delhi. But it was otherwise ordained. As the poet says 'true as the peach to its ripening taste is destiny to her hour.' On the 19th of February, 1915, he died, and of him surely, in another age and in another land were the prophetic words uttered—'Greater love hath no man than this, that a man lay down his life for his friends.'

NOTES

Appreciation: this word originally meant fixing the value of something, valuing; then it came to mean *valuing highly*.
They struck the keynote: they set the tone or fixed the manner.
Exhortation: earnest persuasion.
Flawless: without any mistake.
Relentless: always severe, merciless.
The consummate logic of facts and figures: The perfect arguments which we get from keeping our minds on facts, and not letting the imagination ruin our judgment.
Inexorable candour: unchangeable honesty.
Compromise: settlement of a dispute.
Restraint: self-control, avoiding all excess.
Veracity: true nature.
Self-repressions: acts of self-control.
Urgent: pressing.
Ecstasy: enthusiasm.
The born idealist: the person who by nature always sees things in their best light, or as they might be, rather than as they are.
Disillusion: disappointment.
Strenuous: using much exertion.
Ancestry: his line of forefathers.
Despondent: despairing.
Conviction: feeling sure or convinced about something.

Adulation: flattering praise.
Unanimous acclamation: applause from everybody present.
Scanning: looking through.
Rebellious turban: the turban which must have rebelled against making way for a top-hat.
Rapture: extreme joy, ecstasy. **Signally:** eminently.
Martyrdom: suffering for an ideal. **Concern:** anxiety.
Human situations: circumstances in which people find themselves placed.
Luminous: very bright, illuminating.
Marred: spoilt.
Of absorbing interest: taking up all his interest.
Unison: agreement.
Grapple with: seize and struggle with.
Embodiment: the form which something takes.
Stimulant: a medicine to excite a patient.
Sedative: a medicine to soothe or quieten a patient.
Monotony: sameness, want of change.
Convalescence: coming back to health.
Solaced: consoled.
Arduous: very hard, strenuous.
Dedicated: solemnly devoted. **Scurvy:** mean.

QUESTIONS

1. What does Mrs. Naidu say about her early relations with Mr. Gokhale?
2. Give in your own words an account of Mrs. Naidu's impressions of the personality of Mr. Gokhale on their meeting in Calcutta.
3. What happened at the evening meeting with Mr. Gokhale at the building of the Servants of India Society?
4. What was Mr. Gokhale's beautiful question to Mrs. Naidu and her equally beautiful answer?
5. What examples does Mrs. Naidu give of Mr. Gokhale's striking characterizations?
6. What were the main questions which absorbed the interest of Mr. Gokhale?
7. What impressions do you get from this piece of the character of Mrs. Naidu?

SUBJECTS FOR ESSAYS

1. Devotion to India.
2. The Personality of Mr. Gokhale.

VI

THE ELEVATION OF THE DEPRESSED CLASSES

By G. K. Gokhale

(Speech delivered at the Dharwar Social Conference held on April 27th, 1903).

Gopala Krishna Gokhale was born at Kolhapur in 1866, and graduated at the Elphinstone College, Bombay, in 1884. He lectured at the Fergusson College, Poona, on History and Political Economy, and became principal of the College, retiring in 1902. It was as a member, and secretary and president, of the Indian National Congress, as an expert on Indian finance, as a participator in provincial and central legislature, as a patriot devoted to constitutional procedure, and as the founder of the Servants of India Society, that he made his mark on the history of his country. How affectionately he is regarded may be seen in the tribute which Mrs. Naidu wrote on his death in 1915. It has been said of him that 'his intense patriotism, powerful grasp of facts and great industry raised him head and shoulders above his contemporaries; and his moderation, inevitable courtesy and lofty personal character marked him out as one of the best and greatest of the old school of Congress politicians before the age of Non-co-operation.'

I do not propose to deal with this subject as an antiquarian; I only want to make a few general observations from the standpoint of justice, humanity, and national self-interest. I think all fair-minded persons will have to admit that it is absolutely monstrous that a class of human beings, with bodies similar to our own, with brains that can think and with hearts that can feel, should be perpetually condemned to a low life of utter wretchedness, servitude and mental and moral degradation, and that permanent barriers should be placed in their way so that it should be impossible for them ever to overcome them and improve their lot. This is deeply revolting to our sense of justice. I believe one has only to put oneself mentally into their place to realize how grievous this injustice is. We may touch a cat, we may touch a dog, we may touch any other animal, but the touch of these human beings is pollution! And so complete is now the mental degradation of these people that they themselves see nothing in such treatment to resent, that they acquiesce in it as though nothing better than that was their due.

I remember a speech delivered seven or eight years ago by the late Mr. Ranade in Bombay, under the auspices of the Hindu Union Club. That was a time when public feeling ran high in India on the subject of the treatment which our people were receiving in South Africa. Our friend, Mr. Gandhi, had come here on a brief visit from South Africa and he was telling us how our people were treated in Natal and Cape Colony and the Transvaal—how they were not allowed to walk on footpaths or travel in first-class carriages on the railway, how they were not admitted into hotels and so forth. Public feeling, in consequence, was deeply stirred, and we all felt that it was a mockery that we should be called British subjects, when we were treated like this in Great Britain's colonies. Mr. Ranade felt this just as keenly as any one else. He had been a never-failing adviser of Mr. Gandhi, and had carried on a regular correspondence with him. But it was Mr. Ranade's peculiar greatness that he always made use of occasions of excitement to give a proper turn to the national mind and cultivate its sense of proportion. And so, when every one was expressing himself in angry terms about the treatment which our countrymen were receiving in South Africa, Mr. Ranade came forward to ask if we had no sins of our own to answer for in that direction. I do not exactly remember the title of his address. I think it was 'Turn the searchlight inwards,' or some such thing. But I remember that it was a great speech—one of the greatest that I have ever been privileged to hear. He began in his own peculiar fashion, expressing deep sympathy with the Indians in South Africa in the struggle they were manfully carrying on. He rejoiced that the people of India had awakened to a sense of the position of their countrymen abroad, and he felt convinced that this awakening was a sign of the fact that dead things were once again coming to life. But he proceeded to ask: 'Was this sympathy with the oppressed and down-trodden Indians to be confined to those of our countrymen only who had gone out of India? Or was it to be general and to be extended to all cases where there was oppression and injustice?' It was easy, he said, to denounce foreigners, but those who did so were bound in common fairness to look into themselves and see if they were absolutely blameless in the matter. He then described the manner in which members of low caste were treated by our own community in different parts of India. It was a description which filled the audience with feelings of deep shame and pain and indignation. And Mr. Ranade very justly asked whether it was for those who tolerated such disgraceful oppression and injustice in their own country to indulge in all that denunciation of the people of South Africa. This question, therefore, is, in the first place, a question of sheer justice,

Next, as I have already said, it is a question of humanity. It is sometimes urged that if we have our castes, the people in the West have their classes, and after all, there is not much difference between the two. A little reflection will, however, show that the comparison is quite unfair. The classes of the West are a perfectly elastic institution, and not rigid or cast-iron like our castes. Mr. Chamberlain, who is the most masterful personage in the British Empire today, was at one time a shoemaker and then a screw-maker. Of course, he did not make shoes himself but that was the trade by which he made money. Mr. Chamberlain today dines with Royalty, and mixes with the highest in the land on terms of absolute equality. Will a shoemaker ever be able to rise in India in the social scale in a similar fashion, no matter how gifted by nature he may be? A great writer has said that castes are eminently useful for the preservation of society, but that they are utterly unsuited for purposes of progress. And this I think is perfectly true. If you want to stand where you were a thousand years ago, the system of castes need not be modified in any material degree. If, however, you want to emerge out of the slough in which you have long remained sunk, it will not do for you to insist on a rigid adherence to caste. Modern civilisation has accepted greater equality for all as its watchword, as against privilege and exclusiveness, which were the root-ideas of the old world. And the larger humanity of these days requires that we should acknowledge its claims by seeking to improve the helpless condition of our downtrodden countrymen.

Finally, gentlemen, this is a question of National

Self-interest. How can we possibly realise our national aspirations, how can our country ever hope to take her place among the nations of the world, if we allow large numbers of our countrymen to remain sunk in ignorance, barbarism, and degradation? Unless these men are gradually raised to a higher level, morally and intellectually, how can they possibly understand our thoughts or share our hopes or co-operate with us in our efforts? Can you not realise that so far as the work of national elevation is concerned, the energy which these classes might be expected to represent is simply unavailable to us? I understand that that great thinker and observer—Swami Vivekananda—held this view very strongly. I think that there is not much hope for us as a nation unless the help of all classes, including those that are known as low castes, is forthcoming for the work that lies before us. Moreover, is it, I may ask, consistent with our own self-respect that these men should be kept out of our houses and shut out from all social intercourse as long as they remain within the pale of Hinduism, whereas the moment they put on a coat and a hat and a pair of trousers and call themselves Christians, we are prepared to shake hands with them and look upon them as quite respectable? No sensible man will say that this is a satisfactory state of things. Of course, no one expects that these classes will be lifted up at once morally and intellectually to a position of equality with their more-favoured countrymen.

This work is bound to be slow and can only be achieved by strenuous exertions for giving them education and finding for them honourable employment in life. And, gentlemen, it seems to me that, in the present state of India, no work can be higher or holier than this. I think if there is one question of social reform more than another that should stir the enthusiasm of our educated young men and inspire them with an unselfish purpose, it is this question of the degraded condition of our low castes. Cannot a few men—five per cent., four per cent., three, two, even one per cent.—of the hundreds and hundreds of graduates that the University turns out every year, take it upon themselves to dedicate their lives to this sacred work of the elevation of low castes? My appeal is not to the old or the middle-aged—but I think I may well address such an appeal to the young members of our community—to those who have not yet decided upon their future course and who entertain the noble aspiration of devoting to a worthy cause the education which they have received. What the country needs most at the present moment is a spirit of self-sacrifice on the part of our educated young men, and they may take it from me that they cannot spend their lives in a better cause than raising the moral and intellectual level of these unhappy low castes and promoting their general well-being.

VII

FAREWELL TO FERGUSSON COLLEGE

By G. K. Gokhale

(On the eve of his retirement from the Fergusson College, the students presented Mr. Gokhale with a farewell address, on Friday, the 19th September 1902, to which he replied as follows:)

It is not possible for me to rise without deep emotion to reply to the address which has just been read, and to return thanks for the great, the overwhelming kindness with which you have treated me today. All parting in life is sad, but where the heart's deepest feelings are involved, the breaking of old ties, and the necessity of saying good-bye, is about as trying an ordeal as any that a man can be called upon to go through. For eighteen years now, I have tried, according to the humble measure of my capacity, to give the best that was in me to this Society. Through good report and through evil report, through sunshine and through storm, it has been my endeavour to work for this institution with a single aim to its welfare, till at last it has become impossible for me to think of myself as apart from this College. And now, when the time for my withdrawing myself from all active work in this institution has come, my heart is naturally stirred by conflicting emotions, in which a feeling of intense thankfulness is mingled with a feeling of deep sadness. I feel thankful, profoundly thankful that it has pleased Providence to give it to me to discharge the solemn and onerous obligations of a vow taken so many years ago, under the influence of youthful enthusiasm, and that no matter what happens to me in the future, I shall always be able to look back with pleasure and pride on this part of my career, and say to myself : ' Thank God, I was permitted to fulfil my pledge.' But, gentlemen, side by side with this feeling of thankfulness, there is a feeling of deep regret, that my active work for this great institution is now at an end. You can easily understand what a wrench it must be to me to thus tear myself away from an institution, to which my best work hitherto has been given, and which always has been first in my thoughts and affections, no matter in how many fields it was my lot to work. Some of you here may, perhaps, be tempted to ask, as other friends have already asked,—why do you retire from the College, if you feel the parting so keenly? My answer to this question is, that my decision has not been arrived at without a long and anxious examination of the whole position. In the first place, my health is not now what it once was. During the last term, it was a matter of anxiety to me from week to week, and almost from day to day, how I should be able to finish my work without breaking down in the middle of the term. Even then, as many of you are aware, I was not able to perform my duties in the College with that strict regularity with which my colleagues were performing theirs, and one cannot help feeling that this is a very unsatisfactory position to be in, though never a word of complaint was heard from my colleagues. And I felt I had no right to put a strain on their kindness. You know the golden rule that when you sit down to a repast, it is always well to rise a little hungry, or when you go to a friend's house, you should rather leave before your time than overstay his hospitality even by a day. I know my colleagues do not think that the illustrations apply. All the same, having worked for eighteen years, more or less under high pressure, I thought it was best for me to retire and leave the field to other workers. This, however, is not my sole reason for withdrawing from the College, and some of you are likely to think that it is not a very conclusive one either, and I will frankly tell you that another reason has influenced me in making up my mind, quite as much as this one. Years ago, I remember to have read the story of a man, who lived by the side of the sea, who had a nice cottage and fields that yielded him their abundance, and who was surrounded by a loving family. The world thought that he was very happy. But to him the sea had a strange fascination. When it lay gently heaving like an infant asleep, it appealed to him; when it raged like an angry and roaring lion, it still appealed to him; till at last he could withstand the fatal fascination no longer. And so having disposed of everything and put his all into a boat, he launched it on the bosom of the sea. Twice was he beaten back by the waves—a warning he would not heed. He made a third attempt, when the pitiless sea overwhelmed him. To a certain extent this seems to me to be my position today. Here I am with a settled position in this College, and having for my colleagues men with whom it is a pleasure and a privilege to work, and whose generosity in overlooking my many faults and magnifying any little services I may have rendered, has often touched me deeply. And yet, I am giving up all this to embark on the stormy and uncertain sea of public life. But I hear within me a voice which urges me to take this course, and I can only ask you to believe me when I say that it is purely from a sense of duty to the best interests of our country, that I am seeking this position of greater freedom, but not necessarily of less responsibility. Public life in this country has few rewards and many trials and discouragements. The prospect of work to be done is vast, and no one can say what is on the other side—how all this work may end. But one thing is clear. Those who feel in the matter as I do must devote themselves to the work in a spirit of hope and faith, and seek only the satisfaction which comes of all disinterested exertions. This is not the place where I may speak of my future hopes or lines of work. But one thing I know, and it is this: Whether I am permitted to press onwards and prove of some little use to the public in another capacity, or whether I have to return a weather-beaten, tempest-tost, shipwrecked mariner, my thoughts, as you have said in your address, will constantly be with this institution; and, on the other hand, I shall always be sure of a warm and hospitable welcome within these walls, whenever I choose to come here. And, now, before concluding, I wish to say one thing to the students of this College. I hope and trust that they will always be proud of this institution. I am about to leave you and so I can speak on this subject now more freely and frankly. I have been nearly all over India, and I have naturally felt special interest in the educational institutions of different places. Nowhere throughout the country is there an institution like this College of ours. There are other institutions better equipped, and also with older traditions; but the self-sacrifice of men like my friends Mr. Paranjpye and Mr. Rajawade surrounds this College with a halo of glory all its own. The principal moral interest of this institution is in the fact that it represents an idea and embodies an ideal. The idea is that Indians of the present day can bind themselves together, and putting aside all thoughts of worldly interests work for a secular purpose with the zeal and enthusiasm which we generally find in the sphere of religion alone. The ideal is the ideal of self-help, that we may learn slowly but steadily to rely less and less upon others, however willing to bear our burdens, and more and more upon ourselves. I trust that you, the students of this College, will keep this character of the institution steadily before your eyes—that your devotion to it, your enthusiasm for it, will be commensurate with the nobility and importance of its work, that even when you feel disposed to criticise it, you will speak of it with that loving solicitude with which we mention a parent's faults, and that you will always do what lies in your power to further its interests and enlarge the sphere of its usefulness and influence. And now nothing remains for me but to say 'good-bye.' I know I have given but feeble utterance to the thoughts that are at this moment uppermost in my mind, but nothing that I can say will express them adequately. I wish you well—individually and collectively. In leaving you, as I am doing, I feel I am leaving the best work of my life behind me. I trust I may meet some of you hereafter as co-workers in other fields, that we may also occasionally meet within the walls of this College. God bless this College and bless you all.

NOTES

Antiquarian: one who studies old things.
Monstrous: exceedingly shameful.
Pollution: making a person unclean.
Acquiesce in: agree to.

Auspices: patronage. **Denounce**: accuse.
To indulge in all that denunciation: to denounce or attack them without any restraint.
Exclusiveness: shutting other people out from the enjoyment of certain things.
Pale: bounds. **Single aim**: one purpose.
Onerous: hard, heavy. **Wrench**: painful twist.
Fascination: great charm or attraction.
Heaving: rising in waves. **Exertions**: efforts.
Halo: a light or glory round the head of a saint.
Secular: worldly. **Commensurate with**: equal to.
Solicitude: care, anxiety.

QUESTIONS

A

1. What did Mr. Gokhale say about the injustice shown to the Depressed Classes?
2. How did Mr. Justice Ranade regard the agitation caused by unfairness to his countrymen in South Africa?
3. What illustration did Mr. Gokhale give of the difference between classes in England and castes in India?
4. What were Mr. Gokhale's views about the condition and elevation of the masses?
5. What was the appeal Mr. Gokhale made to the students at the end of his speech?

B

1. Tell what you can remember of the noble words at the beginning of Mr. Gokhale's speech?
2. Summarise Mr. Gokhale's reasons for leaving educational work.
3. What was the analogy Mr. Gokhale used in reference to his entering political life?
4. How did Mr. Gokhale face the strenuous work awaiting him?
5. What was the last wish expressed by Mr. Gokhale?

SUBJECTS FOR ESSAYS

1. The Example set by Mr. Gokhale.
2. Perseverance.
3. The Duties of a Servant of India.

VIII

THE YOUNG ELEPHANT

BY DHAN GOPAL MUKERJI

Mr. Dhan Gopal Mukerji was born in Bengal in 1890 and educated in the universities of Calcutta, Tokyo, California and Stanford. He is a writer who has steadily won renown, first in America and then in England, by his charming stories of Indian village life, and especially of the animals of the jungle. Some of his books are *Caste and Outcaste, Kari the Elephant, Jungle Beasts and Men, Ghond the Hunter, Gay-Neck, the Story of a Pigeon,* and *Chief of the Herd,* another elephant book, from which the following chapter is taken. These are very charming books, and they have attracted much attention from Western critics, who have written such things as the following about them :

> 'The life of a Hindu village is drawn so delicately that the book has a sort of silence in it that is as soothing as it is strange.'

> 'There are passages of great beauty, passionate descriptions, in a language not quite our own. The words are our words, but the imagination that has grouped them is subtly different.'

> 'At the end one has an extraordinarily clear impression of a far and different country, new ideas and standards, and a quite different range of sensibilities. The descriptions of wild life and the jungles of Sikkim are extremely good—the stillness, and then all the quiet noises, the dewy orchards and the great trees dripping with creepers.'

Among Mr. Mukerji's earlier books are three beautiful ones published in San Francisco, *Layla-Majnu,* a musical play, of which Prof. Upham Pope wrote: 'Not only is there here much of the tone of the great Indian classics, but something of the spirit of them is transmitted in a way that wins the favour and sympathy of the reader of a wholly different cultural background. Mrs. Sarojini Naidu's exquisite lyrics in *The Golden Threshold* were written in English; they are excellent English poetry, but the Soul of India has spoken through them. It is this double success of a rare and important kind that Mr. Mukerji appears to me to have achieved.'

Uniform with this play appeared two volumes of poems, both rhymed and in free unrhymed verse—*Rajani, Songs of the Night* and *Sandhya, Songs of Twilight.* They are full of colour, full of heart-felt impressions of beauty, full of poignant memories of youth and childhood, and of sympathy and devotion to the dearest things in life.

THE first night we halted in the delta of the Ganges, the Sundarbans, whose jungles are full of tigers and leopards, and its streams packed with crocodiles. The water was salty, and undrinkable. So we had to dig with our feet in certain places and drink from springs that were a few inches below the earth's surface.

Bahadur's sleeping arrangements had to be quite new this time. He was obliged to sleep in a group with the other babies. Around them we placed, in the form of a ring, all the youngsters below ten. Next to them stood all the mothers of the flock in a circle; these we hemmed in and protected with a ring of boys below thirty years of age, and last of all came the ring made by the adults of the herd standing nose to tail. After having seen to this and taking my place in the ring of the big male elephants, I ordered all to sleep soundly. Nothing untoward happened till sunrise when two hungry tigers circled around us a few times, examining our formation. Soon they tired of this and went off in quest of other things.

We did not keep this formation during the rest hours of the day: instead, the parents, both male and female, watched over their respective children. Sometimes two or three families grouped together and went off by themselves. Generally the children would sleep all in a bunch while the parents stood silent like ebony walls around them. Elephants keep very quiet, not only during the rest hours of infants, but most of the time. This is probably due to our size. Normally we expose so much of ourselves to danger that, in order to keep proper watch over our own safety, we have to listen, look and smell with the utmost stillness. Stillness is our normal environment no matter where we are. Any disturbed surroundings are uncongenial to us.

After they have had their rest, the children play with their own parents. This rule was rarely broken during the first twelve months of a calf's life. After all, the little fellows could not march all morning and all afternoon without some hours of real play. We generally took Bahadur with us and played with him. But one afternoon the parents decided to teach the youngsters how to swim. By this time Bahadur was about three months old. Each child stood between his father and mother, and all of them waited on the river bank for a signal from me. But I could not order them to plunge in without making sure that not only the jungle behind us was safe but also that the water before us was uninhabited by crocodiles and sharks. So I put my trunk into it and took a little water, which I tasted with my tongue. Since it was not salty I decided that there should be no sharks in it. Then, in order to be perfectly sure that there were no crocodiles under the surface lurking to attack us, I buried half of my trunk into its depth and waited. Since no animal bit my nose, though I held it as long as I could, I decided it was safe. Even then the mothers would not let the children go in. So we, the males, swam in a crescent shape half-way across. Elephants do that in order to clear a few yards of water from all animals. When the water-dwellers see such vast shapes plough their world with so many legs, they leave their place to us without much ado. After that we called our wives and children to join us. The infants refused to budge. They preferred the shore to the swim.

Now each father had to go up and coax his child to come down. Our son refused to put a foot off the ground. What were we to do? At last I told him that we were going across the river. This frightened him all the more. Then I pointed to his mother who was floating in the water, which meant that all elephants float. They never drown. Hatis are too fat to sink anywhere. But Bahadur proved obdurate. So his mother came half-way up the shore and put her trunk around him. In the meantime all the other parents had coaxed their infants off the ground. Seeing them floating, and as Radha began to pull him, I pushed Bahadur from behind. In an instant he was in the river. I jumped after him. He tried to balance himself by wriggling his legs, but that made him roll over. I had to put my trunk around his and keep him from putting it into the water. Now he floated evenly and in a few minutes I let go of his trunk but instead of holding it up, he let it sink. In a flash Radha lowered her own and pulled it up. The instant it emerged out burst a veritable fountain of water accompanied by trumpeting.

Again after floating a while, his mother let go his nose. This time too he let it sink. I had to push mine after it, swiftly bringing both of them again into the air. This time he and I both shot out a lot of water. My head fairly ached with pain and confusion. I must say that Bahadur was not a complete duffer, for the third time his nose was released he kept it erect above the water, and thus we taught him how to float in the river. The next day he learned to use his feet properly, and, lo! before the week was out, he was fording rivers with the utmost ease.

Next to conquest of water, the thing that an elephant should know is the conquest of the air. I mean by that that a calf, before he is a year old, should be able to tell by the odour in the atmosphere what animal is passing him.

In the beginning we taught him to divide the odours into two classes—one of the vegetarian, the other of the meat-eating beasts. Next, we taught him to distinguish cats from dogs as the two distinct types of killers. He learned also to distinguish wolves from wild dogs, and leopards from tigers. All this took time to learn. But before he was two years old, Bahadur knew all that there was to know from us about the scent of an animal.

The greatest danger that he ever ran into was when we were teaching him to recognise wolves, leopards, and the cobra. He was almost devoured by wolves one day. It was during the second rainy season of his life. Though it was the season for great downpours, no rain had fallen till July. The whole world was stricken with drought. Brooks dried as fast as a water-drop disappears in sand-hills. Rivers grew thin as an elephant's tail, then stopped running. Trees whose roots did not go deep died in a short time. Grass and reeds throbbed with heat like yellow wastes. Stung by thirst and hunger, we proceeded towards the mouth of the Ganges where there was at least the sea.

But it is the moral law of the jungle that when the drought comes all the animals, whether killers or prey, cease hunting and hurting one another. In the face of a common danger such as drought or flood, the animals do not struggle for existence. They co-operate and foes and friends help each other to escape from the zone of danger.

We made sure, from the birds who spread the news, that this calamity of drought was upon us. They, being used to flying great distances, can tell how far-reaching troubles can be. Then, after they spread the bad news, the elephants who travel nearly as far, for they wander day and night, give the call. Between the birds and the hatis the people who catch the news from below and above are the monkeys. They love to bring and broadcast news. Now all of them, puffed up with self-importance, ran from tree to tree jabbering and screaming: 'Arise, awake, run before you die of thirst!' But the idiots did not tell people which way to run. That is why a general stampede began. It looked as if the whole jungle was to run in all directions at once. The screams of terrified beasts grew horrible. The din of it froze one's hearing. Suddenly a cry lashed the air. It slashed and smashed the other sounds and made them still. 'Bonka, bonok, bawn,' bellowed the wild buffaloes. They alone had the nose for the water; they were shouting for us to follow their lead to the sea. Why is it that the cows are more fitted to find water than any other animal? Of course the birds are the best guide to any place far off, but they cannot tell by the odour of the soil whether there is water under it. Both cattle and elephants can do that. Birds see. We smell. Since their figures of speech are in terms of sight, we do not grasp them.

Hence during our present search for water, the buffaloes had to lead. Their leadership we could understand, for they used their nostrils like the rest of us.

Close behind them followed the tigers and leopards. Next went all the hatis. This was a good precaution, for in case the buffaloes missed the way, our trunks might find water. After us the antelopes, deer, bears, dogs and many other tribes. Thus we marched in the utmost friendliness. We had the monkeys and birds overhead. They, too, kept on moving like the rest, but as one might foresee, many of the monkeys abandoned the quest after several days. I am told that they perished of the drought. Of all the races the Hanumans are most changeable, and that is the reason of their suffering and misery.

After a week's journey we reached a river at least half-full of water. All the animals drank together of its water, clean as the eye of a bird. Oh! what a relief! Every species was filled with joy. After drinking, bathing began. Animal after animal wallowed in the broad shallow river in the very open. No fear of any kind showed itself amongst us. The past few days' friendly intercourse had removed all memories of fear and hate from our hearts.

Alas! no noble emotion prevails long amongst mortals. It was a pack of wolves who rekindled the flame of slaughter toward sundown that day. While Radha, Bahadur and I were eating a few twigs from the neighbouring trees, suddenly we heard the bark of distress from a sambur, a big deer. We looked in vain for him. No matter which way we looked we could get no more sound nor scent of him. My nose told me nothing for a minute or so; Radha too could not tell a thing. But Bahadur's young powerful nostrils told him that a dog or two were drawing nearer. Since he feared no dogs, he went forward in their direction. We followed him at a distance.

No sooner had he taken a dozen more steps than a sambur, red and flaming with sweat, leapt past us. Bahadur trumpeted, saying he smelt more dog. Since dog meant no danger to him, we walked on without haste. We were bent on eating a few more twigs. Then came a ghastly call for help from our son. We ran as fast as we could, but we had to pass between trees which his small body had cleared easily. That took some time. In the meanwhile the trumpets of the boy were drowned by a horrible yell of wolves. Radha, urged by her mother love, smashed half a dozen trees with her head as she flung herself headlong. I followed fast. It seemed as if years had passed before we could reach the howling wolves. There, there . . . what I saw almost froze my blood. Our only son running in a circle before a pack of ravenous howling brutes. They had closed in upon him. 'In one more wink of my eye they will be upon him,' I thought. Radha with upraised trunk, shrilly shouting, ran at them. Her cries did not stop them, but the boy had heard her voice. It nerved him. Instead of running about aimlessly he stopped and trumpeted a challenge. That roar—the roar of a master—held his pursuers at bay for several seconds.

Now in answer to him, I trumpeted back. It was my master call; its pitch makes the whole jungle listen. The wolves turned their heads and instantly took fright. For, behold! Radha was upon them. Her feet kicked them about like pebbles. With a dozen more kicks she cleared a path through them to her son's side. Now the wolves leaped and snapped at her. One of them tore at her trunk. The very sight of it hurled me forward faster. Of course they had been so busy with her that they had not seen me approaching. Like a hill falling with the softness of a sigh but swift as a thunderbolt, I came upon them. I smashed into them with all my might. My four tons trampled dozens to death, yet there were more wolves to kill. They poured at us from every direction. Now I brought my trunk into action; every time one of them leaped in the air, I broke his back with one blow. I swung my nose with as much effect as if it were a hammer. Skulls cracked, ribs broke, and bones were crushed under our feet like river reeds. And still they attacked. Panting, groaning and kicking, I ran round to the exposed side of Bahadur. Seeing that both of his flanks were protected, he stopped trumpeting. Now he too fought. With his little feet he stepped on those who, though wounded, refused to run away. Thus we fought, three to a hundred, ere those dogs would turn tail. At last, after what seemed a long long year of wolf-slaughtering, we found several scores of them fleeing for their lives.

That gave us too a chance to flee the place. It is not pleasant to kill or to inhale the odour of blood. It is sickening. No elephant loves carnage of any kind. Unlike human beings, we do not like waging war. We rushed to the river to wash off all the stains of it from our body. While washing in the cool flood Bahadur avowed that he would never mistake the odour of wolf for that of mere dogs, for mistakes like that are very costly.

Ho! I can hear the question that is rising in your thought. Let me answer it. I can read your mind. You are saying: 'How do odours seem to him?' Well, each odour strikes us differently. For instance, elephants smell vegetarian beasts only very faintly. Buffaloes, stags and sheep smell alike: only in the case of the sheep the odour is very heavy. By the way, you can separate those who eat vegetables from the killers without any trouble. All meat-eating animals smell like dead things. Their odour is not only heavy but foul. To us hatis, meat-eaters are diseased if not deadly.

Of the meat-eaters the cats are different from the dog. The former generally eat only what they kill, but the latter eat what is already dead or killed by another. They smell more foul than the tiger and the leopard. Of all dogs the hyena is easy to recognize by his scent, for he eats nothing but carrion. Dogs and wolves eat less carrion than hyenas, but dogs eat more of it than wolves. That is how one can distinguish the one from the other. To me a dog smells like a rat, and a wolf more like a weasel. Two odours that you cannot distinguish from each other are those of tigers and leopards. They are difficult to separate. Young tigers are easy to tell, for they never eat carrion. Leopards eat carrion occasionally, but do not always succeed in making a kill. So they go about and rob small packs of wolves, cheetahs and young panthers of their prey. If a panther hides his victim anywhere on the ground, the old tigers steal and eat it up. But that only complicates a hati's problem of smelling one kind of cat apart from another. If a young elephant ever brags that he can always distinguish a leopard from a tiger by its odour, be sure that youth is telling a tall story. Don't trust what he has to say. On the contrary you can put your faith in any member of our race who prides himself on telling dogs from cats. That we can do most successfully. Even though they eat carrion, the cats lick themselves, and sometimes they swim in the river and wash themselves clean. Their odour is fresher than the dogs', who are dirtier and eat corpses in any stage of decay, and most of the time smell to Heaven. Their odour is unmistakable.

Here let me say in conclusion that this particular fight with the wolves after our escape from the drought-smitten region taught our son Bahadur not to be too sure of his sense of smell when it was the odours of dogs that were in question. The larger lesson that he learnt was that one should never get between a very hungry animal and his prey unless one is strong enough to fight the aggressor. Lastly he learned how and when all animals co-operate to save every species from a common danger, but that though the killers and the victims co-operate with one another under terrible stress, they return to their old relationship as soon as the common danger is removed. Here men might be superior to beasts. They could help one another so that they need never go back to fighting, killing and war. Man can achieve what beasts do not.

NOTES

Untoward: unlucky.
Normally: generally.
Uncongenial: not to our liking.
Lurking: hiding.
Obdurate: obstinate, impossible to persuade.
Wriggling: twisting from side to side.
Fording: crossing water by walking through it.
Stricken with drought: dried up, so that no water was to be had. *Drought* is connected with *dry;* but *draught* is connected with *draw.*
Wastes: deserts, above which the hot air can be seen throbbing, or trembling.

Calamity: disaster, great trouble.
Puffed up: swollen.
Jabbering: making excited sounds with no meaning.
Stampede: running away to escape.
Quest: search.
Ravenous: very hungry.
Flanks: sides.
Carnage: slaughter.
Carrion: flesh of animals that have died.
Weasel: An animal like a very small mongoose. Such animals, and similar larger ones called stoat, polecat and marten, are all called vermin, because they feed on other animals.
Brags: boasts.
Aggressor: the one who attacks.
Smell to Heaven: smell extremely badly.

QUESTIONS

1. Describe the formation adopted by the elephants at night.
2. What precautions did the elephants take before allowing the young ones to cross a river?
3. How did Bahadur learn to ford a river?
4. What is said about the sense of smell of elephants?
5. What is the moral law of the jungle?
6. Describe the march of the elephants in search of water.
7. Tell in your own words the story of the battle with the wolves.
8. What were the lessons learnt by Bahadur during the drought?

SUBJECTS FOR ESSAYS

1. Human Characteristics of Some Animals.
2. My Own Experience of Elephants.
3. An Indian Story of an Elephant.
4. Write an Account of An Experience of Yourself, or Someone You Know, with:
   (*a*) A Tiger or a Panther.
   (*b*) A Crocodile.
   (*c*) A Snake.

IX

THE WEAVER BIRD

By Salim A. Ali

Mr. Salim A. Ali is a young Bombay naturalist connected with the great Tyabji family, who has devoted his fine qualities of energy, perseverance and passion for accuracy to the study of Indian birds. He is a member and official of the Bombay Natural History Society, one of the best of such societies in the world, and he has written much and lectured much in connection with it. One of his achievements is to have made an independent survey of the birds of the Nizam's Dominions, a labour of love the record of which is being published in the Proceedings of the Society. The following delightful account of the Weaver-bird originally appeared in the *Journal of the Bombay Natural History Society.*

Who has not heard of the Indian baya, or weaver bird, and his pendulous, retort-shaped nests? To look at, the baya is an insignificant little fellow, very similar to the female house sparrow. This, however, is his work-aday attire, in which you see him for several months of the year when he is not occupied with responsibilities of family life. Make his acquaintance again as the monsoon approaches and the choosing of a partner has begun to engage his attention; you will hardly recognise him in his resplendent wedding suit. The rich orange-yellow cap, back and breast, set off by a rakish brown throat-patch running backward through the eye, lend him an altogether distinguished air. His spouse retains the sober raiment of her maiden days.

Bayas are sociable birds. They build in colonies; you may come upon any number of nests—sometimes as many as fifty—hanging from the ends of the fronds of a palmyra.

coconut or date palm or from the twigs of a thorny tree such as the acacia or jujube. What controls the selection of a site is an open question. You may find one palm in a clump hung with thirty nests or more, and perhaps there is no another nest within a radius of a mile. Often the nests hang over water in some old well or small tank. Almost invariably they occupy the eastern side of the tree so that the leafy tree top serves as a bulwark against the southwest monsoon winds, which are severe during the breeding season.

As a keen photographer of Indian bird life, I had often cherished a longing to secure camera records of the baya weavers. Hours spent in watching colonies of these master craftsmen at work had served only to whet my desire to record their fascinating procedure. But the obstacles in the way had been many and varied.

The realization of my desire came as a pleasant surprise. We went to live at Kihim, a delightful little backwater village snuggling amidst dense groves of coconut palms down the West Coast, and here, on one of my birding rambles, I chanced upon a lone acacia tree, standing in the middle of what would in the rainy season be a small lake. The dilapidated old nests that hung from its branches hardly more than fifteen feet from the ground promised well, since bayas not infrequently use the same site for several successive years. It was the torrid month of April: as yet all nature lay under a shroud of dry grass and dust-laden foliage. I decided to bide my time until the cycle of the months should turn the baya's fancies to thoughts of love.

Soon after the coming of the monsoon in June, with its vivifying touch, I eagerly turned my steps toward this acacia, now standing like a sentinel in a little inland sea girt by far-flung paddy cultivation. From a distance the familiar chirruping that marks a colony of baya weavers at work greeted my ears, and the field-glasses proved that my expectations were well founded.

A careful look round suggested the plan of campaign. I returned home in high spirits and got to work. A few straight branches were cut down, and a sort of raised platform about eight feet high was soon rigged up. Next morning I had this carried off to the scene of action and deposited in the knee-deep water opposite the tree and a few feet distant from the nests. I arranged some palm leaves in an upright position around the little platform, behind which I could hide myself unseen. Now I was ready for my vigil.

At first the birds appeared much perturbed by the arrival in the midst of them of this strange hybrid between a stepladder and a palm. To my satisfaction, on returning to the spot next morning loaded with camera and binoculars, I found that the colony had become reconciled to its presence. The splash, splash of my wading through the water caused some alarm, and, by the time I had mounted the platform and settled into position, all the birds had disappeared. Soon, however, they returned one or two at a time, and, though they were somewhat cautious at first, by degrees they resumed normal activities.

Day after day I spent hours, within the seclusion of my hiding place, in watching and photographing the colony a close quarters. Day after day I discovered some new or interesting feature. But let me outline in a general way my experiences of a few hours in this hiding place.

The noise of my progress through the water causes a lull as I arrive at nine o'clock of a fine sunny morning. Many of the birds fly off; a few bolder individuals merely hop away to the other side of the tree. I mount the platform, make myself comfortable on a little wooden stool I have brought with me, and settle down.

The nests are in various stages of construction, but none is more than half built as yet, while in a great many the suspension by which the nest is attached to the twig is just being made. Strangely enough all the workers are adult males in showy breeding plumage. There is one bird to each nest, plying away with bill and foot, now on the outside, now within the inverted basket, or bell. While working on the interior, he perches on the crossbar or loop which is put into the structure immediately after the suspension is made and forms the skeleton of the nest. At a later stage the bottom of this loop is developed to form a partition between the egg chamber and the entrance tube.

Presently a party of birds take wing together to a near-by paddy field, which, I discover, is the source of the raw material. Since the spot is not more than twenty-five yards away, I am able, with the help of binoculars, to watch every movement clearly. A bird alights on the edge of an upright paddy leaf and with his bill cuts a notch about a foot below the tip of an adjacent blade. With a sidewise jerk of his head, he tears off a strip of the required thickness. Holding the strip in his bill, he proceeds to detach another strip and also a third and a fourth. Sometimes the strands are not completely severed at the tip until a tug brings them asunder as the bird flies off. As soon as one bird begins the return journey, the others in the party promptly follow suit. The birds sally forth together and, having hurriedly gathered a few strands, all rush back to the starting point, the fibres trailing behind them in the breeze.

It is an education to watch the little weaver handling his material. There is no halting, no hesitation. He knows exactly what is to be done and how, and no sooner is the material at hand than he proceeds with the structure. The bunch of strips is first roughly pressed down into the site with the bill. They stick to the nest on account of the serrated edges and sawlike roughness of the rice leaf. While they are held with one foot, each strip is worked in individually with the beak—passed under and pulled over—till all are in position. The roughness of the material permits the strips to be pulled in one direction only, and the serrations prevent them from slipping loose once they have been tightly pulled.

I realize by a practical demonstration presently given before me how difficult it is to disentangle strips that have been well woven in. While most of the builders are away on their material-procuring expedition, I discover a laggard in this industrious community. The owner of the nest on which I have photographic designs has gone off; and a neighbour, finding the coast clear, stealthily hops across the unattended nest and tugs at two or three of the interwoven strands. Many hard pulls and jerks are necessary to detach them. The bird proceeds to fly off with the booty, but one of the strips is so stubbornly entangled that, as he flies, he is pulled back and for a moment swings like a pendulum under the nest. My shutter has not been set for speed, and the resulting exposure is a failure. The weight of the robber, assisted by a vigorous flapping of his wings, finally succeeds in getting the strand away, and he hurries to resume work on his own edifice.

I wonder if birds possess anything like conscience. The hurried pulls, the furtive glances around, and the hasty departure all seem very human. A developed picture shows the guilty one busy with three or four of the ill-got strips, little suspecting the forces at work to perpetuate his deed of shame!

He had escaped with the booty a moment before the arrival of the owner, who is the first of the band to return with fresh building material. He finds his nest mauled about, with a few loose strips still dangling below. He also finds his immediate neighbour with a beakful of strips which obviously are not freshly procured, since exposure has already changed them to golden-brown in colour. Beyond looking (or so I imagine) somewhat surprised, Number One takes no action, and, after weaving his fresh strands in, he uncomplainingly proceeds to repair the damage. On another occasion, however, when Number Two, who appears to be a habitual offender, is busy at the filching game, the owner suddenly arrives on the scene. My joy is undisguised. The robber is caught red-handed at last; there is screaming and fluttering, as with claws locked, fighting bill to bill, the two cocks whirl through space, dropping groundward. A few inches from the surface of the water they separate, and each flies amicably back to his respective nest.

Often, after a cock has used up his material, he climbs to the top of the nest—on to the dome—for a breather. I see him constantly tinkering about with the hanging structure, which gradually assumes the shape of a strong rope woven round the extremity of a twig, sometimes for more than a foot in length. When he is perched idly on the nest or not occupied with anything in particular, he continues to weave a fresh strand into the structure or to pull the existing strands tighter. Reinforcing this vital portion occupies much attention; it has to withstand the severe buffeting of monsoon squalls and bear the weight of the family to come.

There is a continuous 'Chit-chat-chit' as work progresses, with an occasional rallying call—a louder and more distinct edition of the same note—which is taken up by the community. The chorus lasts a few seconds and terminates in a long-drawn musical 'Chee-ee-ee' that adds to the liveliness of the colony. Work is suspended while the chorus is in progress, and all the birds join in—whatever the position they may happen to be in at the time—clinging to the nest sideways or upside down or perched on the dome.

Several days go by. The building proceeds apace, but surprisingly enough there are as yet no females on the scene. One morning, however, I see that some unusual excitement pervades the colony. The cause presently reveals itself. A soberly clad female baya is hopping about from twig to twig, followed eagerly by a band of gay cocks, strutting and posturing, first this one, then that, sometimes three or four all at once. The lady looks quite embarrassed by their attentions, which often take so aggressive a form that she is compelled to fly off the tree to save her modesty. She returns again and again, but nothing further happens.

Two days later I am again at my post. Things are now becoming distinctly interesting. Several females are dotted about the tree, all restlessly flitting to and fro with the strutting cocks in pursuit. I wonder what these hens are up to. They are driven off repeatedly by the gushing demonstrations of the cocks, and yet they persistently return.

The next time the cocks fly out to fetch more building material, I shadow the movements of the hens and find them moving about from nest to nest, paying especial attention to any nest nearing completion. At first they sit on the dome; then, gradually entering and perching on the loop, they make a careful inspection. Some of the nests are approved while others are rejected. A baya cock has been known to snip off his half-built nest when it has failed to satisfy a visiting baya hen. In the approved nests, I find the ladies peremptorily deciding to move in; their designs are now unmistakable. They take possession and forthwith commence their self-imposed task of putting the house in order, pulling about and adjusting the strips in the interior of the dome with a proprietary air. The cocks arrive, and, amid the pandemonium, strutting and chasing begin afresh. Some of the hens make off temporarily, but others boldly enter the homes of their choice, even while the cock is outside. In one case two of the hens hit upon one and the same nest. This is the cause of much unladylike language and behaviour.

After the selection of her home, the hen becomes more responsive to the advances of the owner, and soon the couple are reconciled to each other. I now see the hen working within while the cock continues on the outside. Soon after, the eggs are laid.

Three weeks later the scene is still one of bustle and noise, greatly augmented by the incessant cheeping of the young, which now occupy a great many of the nests. The completed nests have entrance tubes from a few inches to more than two feet in length, and a number of cocks now appear solely occupied in elongating them. I see hens constantly arriving with grasshoppers and caterpillars and flying in and out of the tubes. It is a delight to watch a baya shooting up the entrance tube of its nest. The bird comes flying and takes a final dip before it rises vertically upward, gaining the entrance with unerring precision, despite the fact that the tube is hardly more than two inches in diameter and the nest is often swaying violently in the breeze. Each bird invariably flies straight into its own nest, with no hesitation and with never an error of judgment.

The building instinct—mania, one might almost call it—that has come over the cock at this vital period of his life is so strong that, when his nest is taken possession of and occupied by a hen, he promptly begins on a second nest in the same colony. When this reaches a sufficiently advanced stage of construction, another of the wandering female birds—of which there are a number in attendance on each colony at this period—comes along and, like the first, establishes possession. When the egg chamber is completed and wife Number Two is safely on her eggs, the cock goes on to start a third nest. If the building instinct does not die away while he is as yet half-way through the structure, as often happens, this nest may also be appropriated in due course by a third hen ; otherwise it may remain half finished and unoccupied.

This account is the outcome of a two months' close friendship with these delightful birds. The aid of the camera is invaluable : it not only helps you to capture the fleeting moment and thus share your pleasure with others, but also teaches patience and perseverance, the two cardinal virtues for the unravelling of nature's mysteries.

NOTES

Pendulous: hanging.
Retort: a glass vessel used in distilling liquids.
Resplendent: bright, splendid.
Set off: made more striking.
Rakish: smart looking.
Spouse: the female bird.
Fronds: leaves (generally used of ferns).
Palmyra: an Indian palm.
Acacia: a family of trees of which the *babul* is one.
Jujube: It is not known yet what makes the *baya* choose such places for a nest.
Bulwark: protection.
Whet: sharpen, make keen.
Snuggling: lying close.
Dilapidated: fallen to pieces.
Torrid: very hot.
Vivifying: giving life, bracing.
Girt: surrounded.
Vigil: watch.
Hybrid: mixture.
Binoculars: field-glasses.
Serrated: like the teeth of a saw. So we have serrations in 1.16.
Disentangle: *tangle* means hair or thread or string in confusion. *Entangle* means to make into a tangle, or be caught in a tangle; *disentangle* means to set free from a tangle.
Laggard: lazy one.
Pendulum: hanging weight of a clock.
Shutter: a device to close a camera.
Edifice: building, nest.
Mauled about: roughly treated, torn.
Filching: stealing.
Breather: a breath of fresh air.
Tinkering about: patching, improving.
Reinforcing: strengthening.
Buffeting: beating.
Strutting: hopping about proudly.
Posturing: taking up different positions, as if showing off proudly.
Embarrassed: put to shame.
Aggressive: as if they were going to attack her.

Gushing demonstrations: Acting most sentimentally.
Pandemonium: great noise (literally, as of a lot of demons).
Cardinal: most important.
Unravelling: solving.

QUESTIONS

1. Where are the nests of the weaver-bird generally built?
2. Describe Mr. Salim Ali's method of getting photographs of the bayas.
3. How does the baya get material for building his nest?
4. How does the baya actually weave his nest?
5. Tell the episodes of the little robber.
6. What kinds of sounds do the bayas make at their work?
7. Describe the coming and conduct of the hen-birds.
8. How does the baya enter its peculiar nest?

SUBJECTS FOR ESSAYS

1. What this account of the Baya has taught me.
2. A Comparison of Some Indian Birds.
3. The Value of Photography.

X

THE ENGLISH HOME

By A. S. Wadia

Mr. Ardeshir S. Wadia comes from a family whose proud boast it is to have established the first ship-building yard in Bombay, in 1735, and to have built no less than 335 vessels, including many men-of-war, most of them without any European supervision. He graduated with honours from Elphinstone College, standing second on the list, and for a time acted as Professor at that College. He is the author of a number of well-known books, including studies of Moses, Christ, Mohamed, Zoroaster and Sri Krishna. Others are *In the Land of Lalla Rookh*, a delightful tale of travel in Kashmir, and *Reflections on the Problems of India*. Mr. Wadia divides his time between Poona and his English home.

In London, it is said, one need never have an idle moment. This proved only too true in our case : for in sight-seeing, in going to theatres, in visiting friends and picture-galleries, and in taking little suburban trips, the fortnight we were there passed all too swiftly and Christmas-day was almost within sight. So one bright afternoon we left London for our home in the country. What a magical transformation it was, and in how short a time! But an hour ago we were speeding in a taxi to Paddington amid the rush and hurry of an Imperial city and now as if by magic we were transferred to the peace and solitude of an English country-side. There's a healing in the country-air, says a poet; and if ever I felt it, I felt it that afternoon as we alighted at our little village-station and walked home amid the old familiar scenes of six years ago. How well I remembered every curve and turn of that walk! The old stile, the scented pathway, the uneven hedgerow along the road, the dear familiar click of the gate-latch, and the cherry-tree still standing guard by my window as of old. A cheery fire was burning to give me a warm welcome home and to complete it there came the maid with tea and cakes. The following two days we were busy visiting the poor of our neighbourhood and taking them their Christmas-gifts. Mother made the puddings at home and herself collected the woollen odds and ends for the old and feeble. I liked to watch and loved to take part in these dearly-cherished customs of old England and it did my heart good to see the old people receive their anxiously-awaited yearly dues with an old-fashioned curtsy and true gratitude. Long may England preserve these time-worn customs of hers and may no false ideals come to sever the entirely right relations that at present exist between those who have enough and to spare and those who have not and are in want!

When I went to our village-church I found a few ladies busy decorating several parts of it with ever-greens and flowers. The pulpit was allotted to us and we carried out our share of the work as well as we could with holly-leaves and chrysanthemums. That evening we did a cross and several wreaths for the graves by intertwining laurels and holly and ground-ivy round wire frameworks: and then decorated our home,—I giving a touch of the East by making a festoon of holly-berries and hanging it on the lintel of the porch. All this was quite novel to me and yet I found I could enter with the greatest ease into the spirit of it all. Two of our near friends came on Christmas-eve to have a quiet tea with us and that evening we felt the first effect of the War in the absence of the carol-singers. Mother being used to hearing and entertaining them each Christmas-eve all her life, missed them very much, but to me their absence was calamitous, for I lost the opportunity of a life-time. Next morning as we walked out to attend the Christmas-service, a wonderful scene met my eyes. There was not a breath of wind, and a solemn stillness seemed to brood over the face of nature. Every twig and leaf and blade of grass was covered with a thin coating of what looked like fine crystal sugar. I felt as if I were in a dream, walking in an enchanted land, so powerfully did the first sight of hoar-frost affect me. All with one voice proclaimed it a perfect Christmas-morn. The little church was full and the service had already commenced when we entered our pew. I, of course, could not join in the service—though I did in spirit—so remained a silent spectator of it right through. I had a walk by myself up a neighbouring hill after the service, and on coming home soon sat down with Mother to our Christmas-dinner, and well I enjoyed the turkey and the flaming-hot plum-pudding with a twig of holly stuck jauntily on the top!

The next few days passed off quickly enough and merrily besides. One day the Vicar gave a treat to his Sunday-school children. We went and helped him in dressing the Christmas-tree and in the evening waited on the children with tea and cakes. I lighted the candles on the tree and cut the various toys from off it and handed them over to the boys and girls who stood round in a ring, scanning the treasures with eager eyes. On another day we took various things for our Belgians and the poor people were most delighted with what we gave them. We had six of these refugees. A lady gave her cottage rent free and each week a sum of twenty-five shillings was collected in the village for them. Even the poorest contributed their pennies and as I not infrequently accompanied Mother when she went round for collection, I could see from the general condition of their household that every penny they contributed must surely have meant the giving-up of some one or other of their few comforts of life; still, what they gave they gave with right good will.

Believing with Borrow that for a stranger the best way of getting an intimate knowledge of a country and its people is to walk through great parts of it, speaking to people he happens to meet—my days were mostly spent in taking long walks to our neighbouring towns and villages and talking to those whom chance threw across my path. But I forget I have not yet acquainted the reader with the name of our village and the county in which it is located. Hermitage is its name, and the county Berkshire. No more inspiring or more appropriate name could have been given to this retired old-world hamlet, nor could a prettier county or one more English have been selected for it than Berkshire, where the scenery, as Miss Mitford so truly puts it, 'without rising into grandeur or breaking into wildness, is so peaceful, so cheerful, so varied, and so thoroughly English.' I could not exactly trace the origin of the name but the tradition runs that many generations ago when the village was little more than a straggling wood, there lived a hermit in a little sequestered grove of beech and birch to which the neighbouring villagers gave the name of Hermitage. To this day the well from which the hermit drew his water is shown to the inquisitive stranger and the folklore attached to it is narrated to him, namely that whoever throws a stone into it, wishing something while throwing, will have his wish carried out before long. I am sure I must have bungled somehow in throwing the stone when the present owner asked me to do so, for my simple wish of having a drive in her motor-car remained unfulfilled through all the many months I stayed in Hermitage. Taking our village strictly, one could hardly count sixty habitations, cottages and cottage-like houses all told. Yet within these sixty abodes one came across a surprising variety of human beings, for our village stocked all grades of society from common peasants to titled gentry. Mother being the widow of the late Vicar knew practically everyone. And so in a little while I came to form more than passing acquaintance with most of them and by the time I left Hermitage I had a fairly good idea of the varying modes of life and thought of the rich and poor of our little village-world. Two things struck me as singular,—the surprising amount of work which the well-to-do do-nothings put in and the intimate and entirely happy relations which existed between the poor and the rich. To take but the instance of the lady whose activities from morning to night fell within the sphere of my immediate attention, I found she was connected with various little guilds and societies of our own and neighbouring villages, such as the Nursing Association, Girls' Friendly Society, Waifs and Strays Home Committee, etc. Besides, she looked after eight boarded-out Barnardo children, collected funds for our Belgians, and took a sewing-class of our village-girls once a fortnight. But this was not all. Most of her spare time was taken up in attending to the various little calls for help she received from several parts of the country and in visiting and inquiring after the old and needy of our village and neighbourhood. And what little was left of it was employed in collecting various garments or doing them herself for the soldiers, making them into parcels, and seeing personally to their despatch to the Front. All this was a revelation to me! And this came all the more strongly to me as it was so strangely in contrast to the state of things prevailing nearer home, where the ideals of the well-to-do classes are of a totally opposite nature.

This labour of mercy was not all one-sided. The poor paid back their obligations in ample measure by their touching gratitude and the high respect in which they held their benefactors. And it was a pleasure to observe that in spite of their close relations that a fine sense of distance was instinctively preserved by both parties and that there were no attempts at familiarity or obsequiousness on the one side nor loss of dignity and respect on the other. At times I almost felt I saw before me a state of society which the poets have dreamed of and statesmen striven for—a society in which the rich man helped the poor and the poor man loved the rich.

A point about the English home which forcibly struck me was its noiselessness. Every one seemed to walk on tip-toe, talk in undertones and do things silently. This was so strangely in contrast to the open-door life of the East where one is continuously subjected to all kinds of noise all through the day and part of the night. Even in well-regulated Eastern households the servants are habituated to handle things roughly and noisily and the people themselves to walk with a heavy tread and talk in an animated tone. What I could not quite understand about the English people was their constant grumbling about their weather.

What would pass off for mere drizzle in the East they called rain and what they termed 'a regular storm' would be considered little more than a smart showen with us. I wonder what they would do if they were given a week or two of our heavy rains in the middle of the monsoon! I dare say in the country the roads are wet and muddy in winter; but if one has the right boots on, one never need notice their condition. I would often tell these weather-grumblers that it is one of my pet theories that England owes all her greatness to the rigours and uncertainties of her climate. The uncertainties make for that peculiar alertness of mind and body which so distinguishes an Englishman from all other men, and the rigours develop in him that remarkable tenacity of purpose to which he owes his world-wide Empire. Besides, the wet and cold of the outside world make one long for the comforts of home and the joys of its fireside. The hearth is the very heart of an English home. It seems to awaken in one all the qualities one associates with the heart—warmth, geniality, fellow-feeling—in a word, a general flow of soul and spirits. But one has got to live in England to understand the charms of the English fireside. There is nothing more enjoyable than to come home from a long walk, tired and out of temper, pull up an arm-chair and settle down in it for a cup of tea. Nor is there a companionship readier or one more constant than that of the glowing hearth; and many an idle hour in the long winter-evenings have I spent watching the lambent flame of a blazing fire.

It seems that the great idea of an English home is to have everything snug and cosy, and the houses in a village are built of a size and of a height to carry out this basic idea. Being used to the large, high, spacious bungalows of the East, even in the largest of village houses I fancied I saw a kind of giant doll's house. The same is the case with English scenery. England does not pretend to take a man's breath away by opening out to him magnificent scenes of huge mountains and deep valleys and rushing torrents. She has no such ambition. To other and sturdier hands she leaves it to stir his imagination, being content if she can but touch his heart by the simpler charms of her landscapes and the tempting softness of her distances. Poets have sung of her shady lanes and sunny commons and novelists have called in all the resources of their art to describe the loveliness of her wild-flower banks or the beauty of her cultivated fields. However remarkable these features of her scenic beauty may be, they are possessed by other countries equally well with her. But there is one feature which, if not strikingly beautiful at first, is so distinguishingly her own and has such growing charms about it that I have often and often wondered why it should have received but scant attention even in the best of English prose and poetry. I mean her undulating land surface. Up and down, up and down the country seems to roll on and on, now flowing in broad sweeps of waving corn and meadow lands and then breaking in deeper curves of grassy knolls and wooded tops, but still—broad or deep, open or wooded, it is the same moving, ever-flowing surface. No flat lands, no jutting rocks, no unsightly thickets anywhere. All is soft and tender and living—in a word, sweet. Should there be any flat land, there are the hedgerows to take off the flatness, or is there a hard contour in some corner of the spreading landscape, kindly Nature spreads a veil of haze and softens the obtruding angle.

NOTES

Mother: the name he gives to the lady of the house.
Cherished: valued.
Dues: what was due to them.
Curtsy: a salutation made by girls and women, by bending the knees and lowering the body.
Holly leaves: the holly is a dark green, glossy leaf with sharp points, originally used at the winter festival to keep off evil spirits, now merely as decoration contrasting with its bright red berries.
Lintel: horizontal piece of wood over a window or door.
Carol singers: at Christmas time people go from house to house singing carols or songs, and are given food, drink and money.
Hoar-frost: a light white frost that covers the ground without freezing it hard.
Jauntily: giving a jolly feeling.
Scanning: looking at.
Our Belgians: refugees who were driven from their homes in the War.
Berkshire: a small English county near London, to the North-West.
George Borrow: (1803-1881) a famous English novelist who wrote a number of delightful books of travel, on Wales, Spain and Russia, and also well-known books dealing with the Gipsies, such as *Lavengro* and *Romany Rye*.
Straggling: in an irregular line, not clustered close together.
Sequestered: lonely.
Titled gentry: gentlemen and ladies with titles, such as knights or lords and their ladies.
Guilds: groups of people.
Waifs and strays: homeless people.
Barnardo children: Dr. Barnardo was the founder of Homes for orphans in London and other places, where they are trained and educated. In the summer the children are sent out to board with farmers in the country.
The front: the front line of battle in the War.
Obsequiousness: acting in a servile way, like a very grateful servant.
Animated: lively.
Drizzle: very light rain.
Rigours: spells of hard or cold weather.
Lambent: playing about the coals (lit. licking).
Undulating: wary.
Knolls: very low hills.
Contour: outline.
Obtruding angle: corner jutting out.

QUESTIONS

1. What does Mr. Wadia say about the contrast between city and country in England?
2. What were his impressions of Christmas Day?
3. How did the village come by its name?
4. What were the things which struck the author most in English village life?
5. What does the author say about the ideal relations he found between the poor and the well-to-do?
6. In what respect does he contrast English and Eastern homes?
7. What has he to say about English weather?
8. How did he enjoy the English fireside?
9. Summarize his account of English scenery.

SUBJECTS FOR ESSAYS

1. An Indian Home.
2. A Description of an Indian Village.
3. Contrast Mr. Wadia, the Indian Traveller in England with Bernier, the French Traveller in India.

XI

ON RIGHTS AND DUTIES

BY THE RIGHT HON'BLE V. S. SRINIVASA SASTRI

The Right Hon'ble Mr. V. S. Srinivasa Sastri was born near Kumbakonam in 1869, like Mr. Gokhale, of humble Brahmin parents. Like Mr. Gokhale, too, he began his life-work as a teacher, and two years after the foundation of the Servants of India Society in 1905, he became a member, thus pledging himself to a life of poverty, purity and self-sacrifice. He became president of the society on the death of Mr. Gokhale in 1915. The *Encyclopædia Britannica* gives the following brief account of his multifarious services to his country.

'Elected to the Viceregal Legislative Council in 1916, he soon came to the front as the greatest Indian orator of his day. He gave discriminating support to the Montagu-Chelmsford reforms, being a member of the Moderate deputation to England in 1919 and serving on Lord Southborough's Franchise Committee; he was elected a member of the new Council of State when the reforms took effect. In 1921 he served on the Indian Railway Committee; he represented India at the Imperial Conference in London, at the League of Nations Assembly at Geneva, and at the Washington Conference on the reduction of naval armaments. The same year he was called to the Privy Council, being the third Indian to receive this distinction, and was made a freeman of the City of London. In 1922 he was deputed to Australia, New Zealand and Canada to confer with the respective governments as to the best methods of practical interpretation of the resolution of the 1921 Imperial Conference on the rights of citizenship of lawfully domiciled Indians, and he achieved definite results. He was chairman of a deputation of non-official members of the Indian legislature to London in 1923 to support representations made by the Indians of Kenya on their disabilities, and certain disappointments led him some way in the direction of aloofness; but in 1926 he accepted an invitation of the Government of India to be a member of the Indian delegation to South Africa for a round table conference with the Union Government.

'A settlement was reached and with the hearty approval of Gandhi, Mr. Sastri accepted early in 1927 appointment as the first Agent-General to the Government of India in South Africa. He showed great judgment and skill in promoting good will and concord during the two years to which he limited his acceptance.'

The following piece is taken from one of the Kamala Lectures on *The Rights and Duties of Indian Citizens*.

WE now come to an examination of the way in which rights and duties stand to each other. At first sight they contrast sharply, rights being your gain and other people's loss, while duties are other people's gain at your expense. Lawyers say that every right belonging to a man implies an act or forbearance which he can compel from others or the State, and every duty is an act or forbearance which others or the State can compel from him. A closer relation can be seen to exist between the two. They may in fact be the same thing looked at from different points of view. For example, the franchise or the power to vote at a parliamentary election is a right conferred by the law on persons possessing certain qualifications. In our country a man is free to exercise this right or not as he pleases. But there are some countries in which every voter must go to the poll. Failure must be satisfactorily explained or entails a fine. In Australia, which I visited in 1922 to plead for the enfranchisement of our countrymen, the vote was extended to them recently; but it has come as a mixed blessing. Some of them are being hauled up for not exercising the vote and do not exactly thank me for my mission. Whether the law makes it a duty or not, the ideal citizen will spare no trouble in understanding the main issue at an election, coming to his own conclusion, and voting accordingly. Ordinarily the percentage of the voters that go to the polls may be regarded as a measure of the political enlightenment of the community and of its fitness for democratic institutions, for at the very root of democracy lies a faith in parliamentary discussion as a means of settling political questions and making progress in constitutional matters. We got the vote for the first time in 1920. Naturally our people had an imperfect understanding of its value, and too many were dissuaded by the agents of non-co-operation from taking part in the first election. A purely negative campaign like that will never again meet with so much success, for our voters will learn more and more that an election is a time not only for fun and excitement but also for exercise of real political power, slight though it be and shared with a multitude of others. Education, especially elementary education, is another item which is both a right and a duty. If the State—say in England or Scotland—can punish a parent for persistently refusing to send his child to school, the parent in his turn may compel the State to provide a suitable school for his child within a certain distance. How far are we in India from such a state of things, notwithstanding all the fuss that is made about compulsory primary education in certain areas? Our next instance will sound strange in this country. It is taken from the constitution of the new German Republic. One of its basic ideas is that every citizen is bound to do work on the one hand and on the other is entitled to have work found for him or in the absence of work to be maintained at State expense. It would be too much to say that these ideals have been realised or that efficient institutions have been devised to secure them. But they have gained a definite foothold in the minds of those who regulate the activities of the State, and it is only a question of time and opportunity for them to be translated into daily practice. On the other hand, what is the state of opinion in our country? What would happen to the legislator who proposed seriously that every man, howsoever rich, should do some work every day? It need not be manual labour, for now it is admitted everywhere that brain-workers are as useful and necessary to the community as any other workers. Idleness is not censured by our public opinion as anti-social; the fact that some ancestor worked hard in his time is held sufficient to exempt from toil generations of his posterity. One of the merits, not fully understood by the public, of Mr. Gandhi's charka creed, is its universality, that is, its application to the rich as well as to the poor. From this standpoint its error is that it ignores intellectual labour. Still there lies behind it the idea that every one must contribute useful labour of some kind to the common stock of society. The practical consequences of such a doctrine would be so revolutionary that its introduction into our polity would be fiercely and stubbornly resisted by the influential part of the community. Why, beggary is quite a respectable profession among us, and some who practise it assure me that it is even lucrative. We have also that large class of people in picturesque robes, sanyasins and fakirs, who do no stroke of work from day to day, but still think that they have a right to levy a toll on the toil of others. Some of these are really learned and pious people whose teaching and example serve certain spiritual needs of the community. But the bulk of this class, whose number runs into hundreds of thousands, are pretenders, practising beggary under a thin disguise of religiosity. But if work as a duty is not yet recognised among us, work as a right to which the individual is entitled from the State is still the dream of a visionary. Unemployment may be never so acute, but you cannot go to the State and say: 'I am without work and hungry. Employ me or feed me.' Just think how far we are behind those advanced communities in which not only is the State bound to find work for each citizen, but it undertakes to find him the precise work for which he is most fitted and through which he can render the greatest service to his fellow-citizens.

NOTES

Entails: is followed by.
Hauled up: taken before a magistrate.
Issue: point in question.
Polls: voting-places.
Polity: form of government.
Lucrative: profitable.
Levy a toll on: compel payment from.
Religiosity: being religious. This word has a touch of contempt.
Unemployment . . . acute: there may be more people out of work than ever.

QUESTIONS

1. What apparent contrast does Mr. Sastri point out between Rights and Duties?
2. In what cases are they different aspects of the same thing?
3. What does Mr. Sastri read into the proportion of actual voters?
4. What happened at the first exercising of the vote in India?
5. What is the relation between the State and the parent in England with relation to compulsory education?
6. What fact in modern German polity does Mr. Sastri refer to?
7. What according to Mr. Sastri, is the valuable idea behind Mr. Gandhi's creed?

SUBJECTS FOR ESSAYS

1. On Mr. Sastri's 'Way of Looking at the Conditions in His Own Country.
2. Some Things to be Improved in India.
3. On Worthy Work.

XII

THE HUMANITY OF SALADIN

BY SYED AMEER ALI, C.I.E.

The Right Hon. Syed Ameer Ali was born in Bengal in 1840 of a family whose ancestors came from Persia into India in the eighteenth Century. His whole life was spent in the effort to improve the condition of Mussalman communities and interpret the ideals of Islam to the outside world. Afer completing his education in Bengal he went to London and was called to the Bar in 1873. He lectured on Mohammedan Law at the Presidency College, Calcutta, for five years. In 1876 he founded the Central National Mohammedan Association, of which he was the secretary for twenty-five years. For a time he acted as Chief Presidency Magistrate in Calcutta, but resigned to practise at the Bar. He was nominated by Lord Ripon as a member of the Imperial Legislative Council as representative of Muslim interests. In 1884 he was given the rank of C.I.E. From 1890 he acted as High Court Judge for fourteen years, during which time his unrivalled knowledge of Mohammedan Law made his work of the greatest importance. In 1904 he retired to private life and a career as a writer, and settled in England not far from London and Oxford. He devoted himself for the rest of his life to the discussion of Islamic and Indian questions, and by his writings spread a deeper and truer understanding of these great matters among the English-speaking world. His best known works are: *A Critical Examination of the Life and Teachings of Mahomed, The Spirit of Islam* and *A Short History of the Saracens*. This last scholarly book has undoubtedly done more than any other in English to convert Western ideas regarding Mohammedan history, character and ideals, and it is written in a terse, matter-of-fact style which is very convincing. The first extract which follows is taken from the Chapter on the Crusades. The passage on 'Islamic Culture under the Moguls' is part of a long paper in the October 1927 number of the valuable and enlightening Quarterly, *Islamic Culture*, edited by Mr. Marmaduke

Pickthall, the eminent novelist and orientalist, and published at Hyderabad, Deccan.

THE Sultan then turned his attention towards Jerusalem, which contained within its walls over sixty thousand soldiers, besides an immense civil population. On approaching the city he sent for the principal inhabitants and spoke to them in the following terms: 'I know, as you do, that Jerusalem is a holy place. I do not wish to profane it by the effusion of blood; abandon your ramparts, and I shall give you a part of my treasures and as much land as you can cultivate.' With characteristic fanaticism the Crusaders refused this generous and humane offer. Irritated by their refusal, Saladin vowed he would avenge on the city the butchery committed by the comrades and soldiers of Godfrey de Bouillon. After the siege had lasted a while, the Crusaders lost heart, and appealed for mercy 'in the name of the common Father of mankind.' The Sultan's kindness of heart conquered his desire for punishment. The Greeks and Syrian Christians within Jerusalem received permission to abide in the Sultan's dominions in the full enjoyment of their civil rights, and the Franks and Latins who wished to settle in Palestine as subjects of the Sultan were permitted to do so. All the combatants within the city were to leave with their women and children within forty days, under the safe-conduct of the Sultan's soldiers and betake themselves either to Tyre or Tripoli. Their ransom was fixed at ten Syrian dinars for each man, five for each woman, and one for each child. On failure to pay the stipulated ransom, they were to remain in bondage. But this was a mere nominal provision. The Sultan himself paid the ransom for ten thousand people, whilst his brother Saif ud-din (the Saphadin of the Christians) released seven thousand more. Several thousands were dismissed by Saladin's clemency without any ransom. The clergy and the people carried away all their treasures and valuables without the smallest molestation. Several Christians were seen carrying on their shoulders their feeble and aged parents or friends. Touched by the spectacle, the Sultan distributed a goodly sum to them in charity, and even provided them with mules to carry their burdens. When Sybilla, the Queen of Jerusalem, accompanied by the principal ladies and knights, took leave of him, he respected her unhappiness, and spoke to her with the utmost tenderness. She was followed by a number of weeping women, carrying their children in their arms. Several of them approached the Sultan and addressed him as follows: 'You see us on foot, the wives, mothers, and daughters of warriors who are your prisoners; we are quitting this country for ever; they aided us in our lives, in losing them we lose our last hope; if you will give them to us, they can lighten our miseries and we shall not be without support on earth.' Saladin, touched by their prayers, at once restored to the mothers their sons, to the wives their husbands, and promised to treat whoever remained in his power with kindness. He distributed liberal alms among the orphans and widows, and allowed the Knights Hospitallers, although they had been in arms against him, to continue their work of tending the sick and wounded and looking after the Christian pilgrims.

Saladin's humanity was in striking contrast with the brutality of the nearest Christian prince. 'Many of the Christians who left Jerusalem,' says Mills, 'went to Antioch, but Bohemond not only denied them hospitality, but even stripped them. They marched into the Saracenian country, and were well received.' Michaud gives some striking details of Christian inhumanity to the exiles from Jerusalem. Repulsed by their brethren of the East, they wandered miserably about Syria, many dying of grief and hunger. Tripoli shut its gates against them, and 'one woman, urged by despair, cast her infant into the sea, cursing the Christians who refused them help.' Out of respect for the feelings of the vanquished, the Sultan had abstained from entering the city until all the Crusaders had left. On Friday the 27th of Rajab, 583 A.H., attended by the princes and lords and the dignitaries of the empire who had arrived in camp to congratulate him on his victory, he entered Jerusalem. The ravages of war were repaired on all sides, the mosques and colleges that had been demolished by the Franks were either restored or rebuilt, and a liberal and wise administration was introduced into the government of the country, quite different from the rude tyranny of the Crusaders.

From Jerusalem Saladin marched upon Tyre, whither somewhat unwisely the Crusaders whom his humanity had liberated had been allowed to betake themselves. The garrison of Tyre, thus enforced from every direction, prepared for an obstinate defence. It was commanded by Conrad, Marquis of Montferrat, a man of ability and great cunning. He refused to obey the summons of the Sultan to surrender the city, alleging that he was under the commands of a sovereign over the seas. Without wasting time upon the siege of Tyre, Saladin turned aside for a while, and marching along the northern sea-board, reduced successively Laodicea, Jabala,

Saihun, Becas, Bozair, Derbersak, and other strong places still held by the Franks. He set at liberty Guy de Lusignan on his solemn word of honour that he would immediately leave for Europe. No sooner, however, did this Christian knight recover his freedom than he broke his pledged word, and collecting a large army from the debris of the crusading forces and new arrivals from the West, laid siege to Ptolemais. And it was now round this place that the interest of three continents became centred for the next two years.

The fall of Jerusalem threw Christendom into violent commotion, and every effort was made by the ecclesiastics to rouse the frenzy of the people and induce the sovereigns and princes of Europe to embark on another crusade.

Thus ended the Third Crusade, in which an enormous number of human beings perished, thousands of homes both in the East and the West were rendered desolate; Germany ingloriously lost one of her greatest emperors, and France and England the flower of their chivalry. Their only gain was the capture of Acre! . . . .

On the departure of Richard, Saladin rested a while at Jerusalem and then proceeded with an escort of cavalry to the sea-coast to examine the state of the maritime fortresses and to put them in repair. At Jerusalem he built a hospital and college under the direction of his secretary and biographer. He then returned to Damascus and remained with his family until his death on Wednesday the 27th of Safar, 589 A.H. 'The day of his death,' says a Moslem writer, 'was, for Islam and the Mussalmans, a misfortune such as they never suffered since they were deprived of the first four Caliphs. The palace, the empire, and the world were overwhelmed with grief, the whole city was plunged in sorrow, and followed his bier weeping and crying.'

Thus died one of the greatest and most chivalrous monarchs the world has produced. Before his death he distributed large sums in charity among the poor, irrespective of any distinction of creed. The messenger who took the news of Saladin's death to Bagdad arrived there with the Sultan's coat of mail, his charger and one dinar and thirty-six dirhems, which was all the property he left. His character can be judged by the accounts of his contemporaries, who describe him as tender-hearted, kind, condescending and affable, full of patience and indulgence. 'He befriended the learned and the virtuous, admitted them into his society, and treated them with beneficence.' No man with any talent ever left his court without some mark of recognition. He covered his empire with colleges and hospitals. The Sultan's vizier, al-Kazi ul-Fazil, who held office under three sovereigns, vied with his master in the patronage of learning and arts. Saladin's council was composed not only of warriors like Karakush, Husam ud-din, Mashtub, but men of letters like the Kazi, the Katib Imad ud-din, surnamed Aluh (the Eagle), who was the Sultan's Secretary of State, the jurist, al-Hakkari, who often exchanged the flowing robes of his profession for a soldier's uniform, and many others.[1]

[1] The famous traveller, Abdul Latif, who saw Saladin after the peace with Richard, speaks of him in the most enthusiastic terms as a great sovereign, whose countenance 'inspired love and respect in every heart.' 'The first evening I spent in his company,' he continues, 'I found him surrounded with learned men who discoursed on every branch of learning. He listened to them

NOTES

Effusion: pouring out, shedding.
Fanaticism: a fanatic is a person who is extremely or even excessively attached to some aim or belief.
Godfrey de Bouillon: (1060-1100) a French nobleman who was a leader in the First Crusade. **Stipulated:** ordered, agreed.
Ransom: a sum paid to set free a prisoner.
Provision: arrangement.
Dinar: a gold coin corresponding to the Indian gold mohur.
Clemency: mercy.
Molestation: interference and injury.
Knights Hospitallers: a great religious order of the 12th century, founded for charitable work.
Ravages: devastation, destruction.
Betake themselves: go.
Reduced: conquered.
Debris: (pron. daybree) fragments, those soldiers who were left after much fighting.
P. 129, l. 8. People in Europe, Asia and Africa were centring their interest on that place.
Ecclesiastics: church authorities.
Bier: frame on which a dead body is carried.
Chivalrous: full of chivalry, the noble spirit of knighthood, which included bravery, courtesy and honour.
Coat of mail: a coat of armour composed of rings or chain-work.
Charger: horse.
Dirhems: a small silver coin worth about four annas.
Condescending: not proud, kind to inferiors.
Affable: willing to talk with others, courteous.
Beneficence: generosity. (not to be spelt *beneficience*)
Vied with: rivalled.
Farriers: smiths who shoe horses.

---

with pleasure, and frequently joined in the discussion himself. He was engaged just then in building the walls and a moat round Jerusalem. He superintended the work personally, and often carried the stones on his own shoulders. He went to the place before sunrise, and returned for breakfast at noon, after which he rested. Later he rode again to the spot and returned only by torch-light. He spent the great part of the night in transacting the business of the next day.' The same writer describes the solicitude of Saladin for his soldiers, and says that at the camp before Acre the market occupied a vast space of ground, and contained over seven thousand shops besides booths and tents for farriers, and one thousand baths.

QUESTIONS

1. What was Saladin's offer to the inhabitants of Jerusalem and how was it received?
2. Summarize the author's account of the Sultan's clemency on capturing Jerusalem.
3. What happened on the Sultan's entry into the city?
4. What does the author say about Guy de Lusignan?
5. How does the author sum up the character of the Sultan?
6. What account does the traveller Abdul Latif give of Saladin?

SUBJECTS FOR ESSAYS

1. The Indian Ideal of a Good King.
2. Religious Unity.
3. The Evils of War.

XIII

ISLAMIC CULTURE UNDER THE MOGULS

By Syed Ameer Ali, C.I.E.

The accession of the Mogul dynasty to the Empire of India marked a new epoch in the history of Islamic culture.

Zahir-ud-din Mohammed Babar, the Lion King, was one of the most remarkable personalities of that age. He began his career at the age of twelve, fighting for kingdoms and losing them. At the age of 37 he acquired Kabul, of which he and his successors retained possession until the time of Nadir.

His *Memoirs* record the story of his life with a simplicity and vividness of description that have few equals in the life-accounts of monarchs. An English writer describes him as a great general and a profound politician. He was an accomplished scholar and versed in Arabic, Persian and Hindi, a curious and exact observer of the facts of every region he entered. He is described as good-humoured, brave, munificent, sagacious and frank in his character.

'The great charm of the work', adds this critic to whom I have referred, 'is in the character of the author, whom we find, after all the trials of a long life, retaining the same kind and affectionate heart, and the same easy and sociable temper with which he set out in his career, and in whom the possession of power and grandeur had neither blinded the delicacy of his taste nor diminished his sensibility of the enjoyment of nature and imagination'

Babar was born in 1482 and died in 1530. He entered India in November 1525 and in less than six months, by the overthrow of Ibrahim Lodi, the Afghan King of Delhi, was master of Hindustan.

The five years of Babar's reign were occupied in conquering the turbulent elements in the country and restoring order; yet, in spite of incessant labour and frequent marches in pursuit of rebels and enemies, he was busy with the creation of aqueducts, reservoirs, and other improvements, and the introduction of new fruits and products from foreign lands. In the midst of his unceasing activities he did not neglect literature: himself an accomplished writer and poet in two languages—Turkish and Persian—he cultivated the society of cultured scholars.

Babar was extremely severe in repressing any excesses on the part of his soldiery. He says himself that having learned that the troops had behaved badly towards the inhabitants of Bahrah, and were 'using them ill' he sent out a party and seized a few of the culprits 'that had been guilty of excesses'; some were executed, others received condign punishment.

Artillery does not seem to have been in use in India before Babar's time. Matchlocks and flintlocks had been employed by the Mameluke Sultan Baibars, surnamed Bandulkdar, to crush the Mongols, but there is no verified record of their being used for purposes of warfare by Indian armies.

The use Babar made of his artillery in fighting with the Indian armies marked an epoch in the history of warfare in that country.

Although he had conquered India he was not particularly

fond of the land and he was full of all the prejudices of a Westerner. The following description is interesting:

'Hindustan is a country', he says, 'that has few pleasures to recommend it. The people are not handsome. They have no idea of the charms of friendly society, of frankly mixing together, or of familiar intercourse. They have no genius, no comprehension of mind, no politeness of manner, no kindness or fellow-feeling, no ingenuity or mechanical invention in planning or executing their handicraft works, no skill or knowledge in design or architecture: they have no good horses, no good meat, no grapes or musk melons or other fruits, no ice or cold water, no good food or bread in their bazaars, no baths or colleges, no candles, no torches, not a candlestick. Instead of a candle and torch, you have a gang of dirty fellows whom they call *deutis* who hold in their left hand a kind of small tripod, to the side of one leg of which, it being wooden, they stick a piece of iron like the top of a candlestick; they fasten a pliant wick of the size of the middle finger, by an iron pin, to another of the legs. In their right hand they hold a gourd, in which they have made a hole for the purpose of pouring out oil in a small stream, and whenever the wick requires oil, they supply it from the gourd. Their great men kept a hundred or two hundred of these *deutis*. This is the way in which they supply the want of candles and candlesticks. If their emperors or chief nobility, at any time, have occasion for a light by night, these *deutis* bring in their lamp, which they carry up to their master, and there stand holding it close by his side.'

Babar died before he had completed his work. His successor, Humayun, did not possess either his military genius or administrative capacity. An amiable and kind-hearted king, he was unable to cope with the turbulent elements of the country, and before long had to leave Hindustan to a new Afghan chief of the tribe of Sur, who, under the title of Sher Shah, united afresh his unruly fellow-countrymen and in 1542 made himself the ruler of Northern India. Sher Shah and his sons held power for nearly 15 years.

Sher Shah's principal reforms were directed to the revival of the rules originally laid down by Firoz for the protection of the agriculturists. The land throughout the country was divided into fiscal units, in each of which he placed five officials, one of whom was a Hindu accountant and another a Mussulman judicial officer. These two acted as the mediators between the revenue officials and the ryots. The system of assessment was simplified, and the new taxes that had grown up since the death of Firoz were abolished. Save in frontier districts and jungle tracts, people were not allowed to keep or carry offensive weapons. He caused a highroad to be made from the easternmost districts of Bengal to the Punjab, planted on each side with shady trees, mostly mango or tamarind. This road was regularly patrolled and was provided with police outposts and *serais* at regular intervals. This road is still in existence. He made three other roads for travellers and merchants as well as the rapid transit of troops; one from Agra to Burhanpur in the Deccan, the other across Rajputana, and the third from Lahore to Multan.

Humayun, hard pressed in India by his Afghan foes and prevented from entering Kabul by his traitorous brothers, betook himself to Persia. Shah Tahmasp the Great was at that time the ruler of Iran, and the magnificence and culture of his Court were a revelation to the son of Babar. On his return from Persia to Kabul five years later he was not only accompanied by a large Persian force to help in regaining his Afghan dominions, but also by a number of men of learning who followed him to India. From that time there was a constant influx of Persian scholars, Persian architects, and Persian adventurers into Hindustan. Persian culture from this reign had a far greater influence in moulding Indian Mussalman civilization than at any previous period of Indian history. And the comparison of that influence with British work within the last century and a half forms an interesting historical study.

Akbar ascended the throne in 1556 at the age of fourteen under the guardianship of Bahram Khan, a trusted servant of Babar. Three years later he assumed the direct rule of his empire. From that time forward the marvellous genius of the young king was employed in suppressing rebellions, consolidating the disintegrated provinces, bringing order out of chaos, and in creating a nation out of the opposing elements of Hindustan. His attempt to unite the Hindus and Mohammedans led to the establishment of a new cult which was hoped to bring into one fold the followers of the two faiths.

His rules and regulations for the government are embodied in the remarkable work called the *Aini-Akbari, The Ordinances of Akbar.* No detail of administration has escaped notice, while the revenue system, based on Khwaja Ahmed Hasan Majmandi's and Firoz Shah's system, is Akbar's greatest legacy to succeeding rulers—a legacy on which the British Government is still working. The *Aini-Akbari* like the *Akbar-nama*, is the work of

Abul Fazl, unquestionably the most gifted and far-sighted of all Akbar's councillors. Akbar was a genius, but probably his labours for the people entrusted to his care would have ended in failure but for the support and unflinching loyalty of a man like Abul Fazl and his brother Faizi.

Nothing shows so clearly Akbar's anxiety for the welfare of the workers on the land or the necessity of making their burdens as light as possible as the minute instructions embodied in the *Aini-Akbari* for the guidance of the collectors of revenue. The village officials of the present day are the descendants of the officials of Akbar's time; the *Kanungo* and the *Patwari* still perform the same duties; they still prepare the *Jummabandis* (the Collector's registers), the *Jummawasil-bakis* (the balance-sheets of the village collections); the rate of rent is still the *Sharh*, the standard of land measurements is still the *gaz* and the advance to the raiyats is still the *takawi*, the old Arabic word handed down from the Abbaside rule in Mesopotamia.

For the purpose of philosophical and religious discussions, at which he was almost invariably present, Akbar erected a special building which was named the *Ibadat-Khaneh* or House of Devotion, where learned men versed in all departments of knowledge, theologians, scientists, poets, travellers, assembled regularly on Thursday evenings.

In Akbar's time tobacco was first introduced into the Mogul capital. There is a quaint account of its introduction in the *Wikaya* of Asad Beg who was sent on a mission by Akbar to Adil Khan or Adil Shah of Bijapur:

'In Bijapur I had found some tobacco. Never having

seen the like in India, I brought some with me, and prepared a handsome pipe of jewel work. The stem, the finest to be procured at Achin, was three cubits in length, beautifully dried and coloured, both ends being adorned with jewels and enamel. I happened to come across a very handsome mouthpiece of Yeman cornelian, oval-shaped, which I set to the stem; the whole was very handsome. There was also a golden burner for lighting it, as a proper accompaniment. Adil Khan had given me a betel bag, of very superior workmanship; this I filled with fine tobacco, such that if one leaf be lit the whole will continue burning. I arranged all elegantly on a silver tray. I had a silver tube made to keep the stem in, and that too was covered with purple velvet.

'His Majesty was enjoying himself after receiving my present, and asking me how I had collected so many strange things in so short a time, when his eyes fell upon the tray with the pipe and its belongings; he expressed great surprise, and examined the tobacco which was made up in pipefuls; he enquired what it was and where I had got it. The Nawab Khan-i-Azam replied: "This is tobacco, which is well known in Mecca and Medina, and this doctor has brought it as a medicine for Your Majesty." His Majesty looked at it and ordered me to prepare and take him a pipeful. He began to smoke it, when his physician approached and forbade him doing so. But His Majesty was gracious to say that he must smoke a little to gratify me, and taking the mouthpiece into his sacred mouth drew two or three breaths. The physician was in great trouble and would not let him do more. He took the pipe from his mouth and bid the Khan-i-Azam try it, who took two or three puffs. He then sent for his pharmacist and asked what were its peculiar qualities. He replied that there was no mention of it in his books but that it was a new invention and the stems were imported from China, and the European doctors had written much in its praise. The chief physician said: "In fact this is an untried medicine, about which the doctors have written nothing. How can he describe to your Majesty the qualities of such unknown things? It is not fitting that your Majesty should try it." I said to the chief physician: "The Europeans are not so foolish as not to know all about it; there are wise men amongst them who seldom err or commit mistakes. How can you, before you have tried a thing and found out all its qualities, pass a judgment on it that can be depended on by physicians, kings, great men and nobles? Things must be judged according to their good or bad qualities and the decision must be according to the facts of the case." The physician replied: "We do not want to follow the Europeans and adopt a custom which is not sanctioned by our own wise men, without trial." I said: "It is a strange thing, for every custom in the world has been new at one time or other; from the days of Adam till now they have gradually been invented. When a new thing is introduced among a people and becomes well known in the world every one adopts it; wise men and physicians should determine according to the good or bad qualities of a thing: the good qualities may not appear at once. Thus the China root, not known anciently, has been newly discovered and is useful in many diseases."

'When the Emperor heard me dispute and reason with the physician he was astonished, and being much pleased gave me his blessing and then said to Khan-i-Azam: "Did you hear how wisely Asad spoke? Truly we must not reject a thing that has been adopted by the wise men of other nations merely because we cannot find it in our books; or how shall we progress?"'

Akbar revived in his Court the institution of ladies' bazaars which flourished in Transoxiana. It was called the *Mina Bazar*, or the Fancy Fair. In these bazaars beautiful stalls were set up for the royal ladies and the wives of nobles and magnates to sell fruits, flowers, embroidery worked by themselves, jewellery and such wares. These bazaars were naturally not open to the general public, but the Emperor, the princes of the royal family and privileged nobles were admitted. The wares, of course, were sold at fabulous prices and the return went to charity.

Many works in Arabic, Persian, Sanscrit, and the languages of Europe were read to the Sovereign. If he did not understand the language, the work was translated for him. The *Singhasan Batisi*, the story of the legendary Hindu king, Vikramaditya, was rendered into Persian by Badauni himself and received the name of *Kherad Afroz*. The Mahabharata, the Ramayana and other old Sanscrit works were similarly rendered into Persian.

The three great men who deserve prominent notice in Akbar's reign are Abul Fazl, the great *Allami* (the scholar, par excellence), his brother Faizi and the Rajah Todarmal, the Finance Minister.

The great work Abul Fazl did to make Akbar's reign a success can never be overestimated nor can the value of Todarmal's revenue administration be overlooked. Abul Fazl and Todarmal are justly regarded as two of the greatest statesmen of any age.

To Akbar, besides Fatehpur Sikri and other cities, we owe the establishment of Allahabad (which Badauni calls Illahabas), not far from the ancient Hindu city of Prayag. The immense garden which his grandson Khusru made there is still in existence.

A sketch of Islamic culture in Akbar's time would hardly be complete without some reference to his clever and accomplished aunt, Gulbadan Begum, the sister of Humayun, a translation of whose memoirs has been recently placed before the public by the industry of Mrs. Beveridge. Gulbadan Begum and Nawab Salima Sultan Begum twice voyaged to Mecca, in those days—when the Indian Ocean was infested by Portuguese pirates —an enterprise attended with extreme danger and difficulty.

Akbar died in 1605 and was succeeded by his son Selim who assumed the title of Jahangir. Jahangir's character was a strange mixture of good and bad. A disobedient son who broke the heart of his mother, a Hindu Rajput lady, and drove her into an early grave, who twice rebelled against an indulgent and loving father, Jahangir when he succeeds Akbar on the throne expresses unbounded admiration for his father's work, a touching devotion to his mother's memory. He took for his administration the ideal of his father's life. Cruel when in drink, he was generous and even mild when sober. He was a good judge of pictures and could distinguish the work of any that came before him.

His marriage with Nur Jahan may be regarded as his salvation, for she weaned him from drink. He saw her first when she was a girl of fourteen at one of the Fancy Bazaars, and his interest grew into love as he saw her from time to time when she came with her mother to visit the palace. Selim's infatuation was brought to the notice of Akbar, who advised Meherunnissa's father, Khwaja Gyas, to marry her off as quickly as possible. She was accordingly married to an Afghan officer who went on duty to Bengal. The story of her husband's death forms a matter of charge against Jahangir's memory, but one can hardly believe that he could have instigated it, as some historians mention, when we remember that for three years after Meherunnissa came to Delhi to take up her residence in the palace, she was absolutely ignored by Jahangir. It was the sight of her at one of the palace functions which revived the old love. At first she refused to marry Jahangir, but at last after great persuasion she consented. She received the title of Nur Mahal or 'Light of the Mahal'. Afterwards the title of Nur Jahan was conferred on her and she is known in history under that name. This lady, though only a queen consort, exercised a far greater authority than the Emperor himself; some coins bore her name also, nobles attended regularly to make their obeisance to her, and she always appeared seated at the window of the palace when the Sovereign showed himself to his people. The regular appearance of the emperor in the morning at the window to show himself to the public was one of the duties imposed on him. Absence from the window generally awakened a fear that the king was no more. Nur Jahan was indeed a remarkable woman. A Persian by birth, she not only spoke but wrote in Persian fluently, and she also spoke the vernacular which had grown up in India.

'It is impossible to describe the beauty and wisdo

of the Queen. In any matter that was presented to her, if a difficulty arose, she immediately solved it. Whoever threw himself upon her protection was preserved from tyranny and oppression ; and if ever she learnt that any orphan girl was poor and friendless she would arrange a marriage for her, and give her a wedding portion. It is probable that during her reign no less than 500 orphan girls were thus married and portioned.' In archery she excelled many practised archers and was a splendid shot; Jahangir mentions in his memoirs that once out hunting with him she killed a tiger at the first shot.

The culture of India, as a whole, bears the mark of her genius. She and her mother invented that beautiful perfume, the *attar* or Otto of Roses; she introduced the fashion of long trains (the *Peshwaz*) for ladies' dresses and the table decorations at banquets were the outcome of her extraordinary faculty.

In Jahangir's time flourished two of the most noted painters that India has produced, viz., Abu'l Hasan, who bore the title of Nadir-uz-Zaman, and Mansur, whose title was Nadir-ul-'Asr. In his *Wakiat* Jahangir speaks in the highest terms of their talents. He also gives an enumeration of the rules he introduced in order to improve the administration. Some were undoubtedly new; others appear to be a re-enforcement of regulations made by Akbar. In the first place he prohibited all illegal cesses levied in any form or under any name by the officers of the State or Jagirdars. He abolished all transit duties on merchandise coming from Kabul to Hindustan or going from one province to another. He directed that the inheritance of Hindu as well as Mussalman deceased persons should descend to their heirs according to their laws. In case no heir was forthcoming, officers specially appointed for the purpose were to take charge of the deceased's property and apply it in building mosques and *serais*, in repairing broken bridges, and in digging tanks and wells.

He prohibited all punishments on criminals by mutilation.

All forcible acquisition of lands or any other property by Government officers was strictly prohibited. He ordered the erection of hospitals in all towns, at which physicians were to be employed at Government expense to attend the sick.

He also prohibited the public sale of intoxicants.

He set free all prisoners who had been in jail with or without trial for any length of time.

Nur Jahan disappears from history on the accession to the throne in 1626 of the brilliant Prince Khurram who assumed the title of Shah Jahan.

Mussalman culture in India attained its zenith under Shah Jahan. He had been brought up by Akbar's eldest wife, Rukaiya Begum, and from the fifth year of his age till Akbar's death he had been the companion and associate of his grandfather. He had imbibed all the high ideals of Akbar. Of a sterner mould than Jahangir, immediately on his accession (1628), he made the Court less brilliant than it was under his more easy-going father. Himself by no means a mean scholar, lavish in his patronage of learning, he gathered round him a galaxy of poets, scientists, litterateurs, and Mussalman divines. In his treatment of the Hindus he did not deliberately offend the prejudices of the Mussalmans, and tried to hold evenly the balance between them, with the result that the best hearts of the empire gave their devotion to him. The history of Shah Jahan has been written by four contemporary writers; we have in them a detailed account of the events of his reign. One of the most interesting among these is the work of a Hindu, Rai Bhare Mal, who held the post of Diwan under Dara Shikoh, the eldest son of Shah Jahan. He thus describes the prosperity of the country during Shah Jahan's reign: 'The means employed by the Emperor in these fortunate times to protect and nourish his people; to punish all kinds of oppressive evil-doers; his knowledge of all subjects tending to the welfare of his people; his impressing the same necessity upon the revenue functionaries and the appointment of honest and intelligent officials in every district; his administration of the country, and calling for and examining annual statements of revenue, in order to ascertain what were the resources of the empire; his issuing stringent orders to the officers appointed to the charge of the Crown and assigned lands to promote and increase the welfare of the tenants . . . . and constantly diverting his generous attention towards the improvement of agriculture and the collection of the revenues of the State—all these contributed in a great measure to advance the prosperity of the Empire.'

This writer goes on to add that, owing to the great regard shown by the Emperor towards the promotion of the national wealth and the general tranquillity, the people had no motive 'for committing offences against one another and breaking the public peace.' Cases were always tried on the spot by the local authorities 'in agreement with the law officers.' If any individual was dissatisfied with the decision he had a right of appeal to the Governor or the *Diwan* (Chief Revenue officer associated with the Subedar for the civil and revenue administration of the District), or to the *Kazi* of the *Suba*[1] who reviewed the matter and gave judgment 'with great care and discrimination.' If parties were still not satisfied, they appealed to the Chief *Diwan* or to the Chief *Kazi* on matters of law, and the cases were further enquired into. The Emperor's own Court was open every Wednesday for the hearing of plaints. But the chronicler says the Emperor often complained in his presence that in spite of all publicity not even twenty plaintiffs ever came forward to apply for adjudication of their cases by the Imperial tribunal. In his Court, the Emperor presided himself assisted by the *Sadr-i-Jahan*,[2] and a few other councillors.

Shah Jahan abolished the ceremony of bending low to the ground which Akbar, in imitation of the Hindu kings, had introduced into his Court, and the usual mode of salutation by bowing was re-established accompanied by raising the hand not once, as was the rule in other Islamic countries, but three times in succession to the forehead.

The Hindustani language attained in this reign its full dignity; it now received the name of *Zaban-i-Urdu-i-Mualla*, the 'language of the Imperial Camp' (Court) or shortly Urdu. Urdu is the same word as *horde*, and means an army or camp. We all have heard of the Golden Horde, which does not mean that it was a crowd of savage Cossacks, but the royal court of the Mongol sovereign.

Shah Jahan's queen, who lies buried under the beautiful dome of the Taj at Agra, was one of the

[1] Chief Justice of the Province.
[2] Lord Chief Justice of the Realm.

sweetest women of whom we have any record in Indian history. Her name before marriage was Arjumand and she was a niece of Nur Jahan. Prince Khurram had fallen in love with her at one of the *Mina Bazars* when they were only 16 and 14 respectively. They were betrothed shortly after, and Jahangir had himself placed the ring on his future daughter-in-law's finger. (The betrothal ceremony is called *Mangni* among the Mussalmans of India and is performed among the upper classes with considerable ostentation.) They were married five years later when she received the title of 'Mumtaz Mahal,—The exalted Lady.' It was essentially a love marriage, so rarely known in the East. Mumtaz Mahal never left his side through all the vicissitudes Shah Jahan went through in his father's lifetime, and his devotion to her was an inspiring feature in his character. With her exquisite beauty she combined an incomparable sweetness of nature. She built and endowed several mosques, *khankahs*,[1] colleges and alms-houses. Her charity was unlimited and both Mussalmans and Hindus received her bounty. Poor girls and helpless orphans were the objects of her special benefaction. She provided dowries for poor people's daughters. Her charity made her name a household word in the Empire of Shah Jahan, and Mumtaz Mahal was soon converted or corrupted into Taj Mahal. And it is by this name that the beautiful mausoleum her bereaved husband raised over her grave is now known. To describe the Taj is absolutely impossible; it symbolises the poetry of architecture and embodies in marble the undying love of a king.

---

[1] Monasteries.

All Shah Jahan's children were born of Mumtaz Mahal—four sons and two daughters; of the latter, the eldest, Jahanara, otherwise called Kudsiya, the 'venerated' Badshah Begum, was a woman of great attainments. Her letter to Aurungzeb to recall him to the duty he owed to their father is a composition of rare merit. She failed. The rest is a matter of history. Aurungzeb, taking advantage of Shah Jahan's illness, marched against his brother Dara Shikoh who had been nominated by Shah Jahan as his successor, defeated him, deposed his father and seized the throne of Delhi. Shah Jahan's reign extended to thirty-two years. He lived ten years longer as a state prisoner of his unfilial and ungrateful son.

Ali Mardan Khan, flying from Persia, took refuge in the Court of Shah Jahan and attained high distinction. He built under Shah Jahan's instructions the splendid Bazaar at Kabul which was afterwards destroyed under Lord Ellenborough's orders. He also constructed 'a canal from the place where the river Ravi descends from the hills into the plains to conduct the water to Lahore', which brought into cultivation a large tract of country.

Aurungzeb's reign was a distinct setback to Mussalman culture. It meant the revival of all that Akbar and Shah Jahan had endeavoured to remove. Mussalman development flowed back into the old channels. The ultra-orthodox historians have lauded his extreme piety, his religious zeal, his obedience to the *Shari'at* (the sacred law), but they have omitted to notice that in fifty years he undid the work of a century; he reimposed the capitation tax on Hindus, which alienated them from the throne, pulled down many of their temples, and completely estranged the Rajput Rajas, who since Akbar's time had been the great supporters of the Mogul dynasty.

What the condition of Delhi was towards the close of the Eighteenth Century is best described by the poet Sauda who died at Lucknow in the reign of Asaf-ud-dowla. In his *Kasidai-Shahr-Ashob* he bewails the fate of this city,—the home of culture, the abode of learning, the shelter of the poor. Addressing the city by the name which it bore after Shah Jahan beautified it with those exquisite architectural works which still delight the eyes of the foreign traveller—Shah Jahanabad—The city of Shah Jahan—he says :

> 'Jahanabad never deserved this cruelty
> But perhaps sometimes this city was the heart of a lover,
> That the lover's image has been wiped out as false.'

Sauda, Atish and several other writers and poets figure in Shuja-ud-Dowla's and Asaf-ud-Dowla's time.[1] The Persian traveller, poet and philosopher Hazin lived in Lucknow and enjoyed the hospitality of Asaf-ud-Dowla. We know something from English writers of this ruler's character and habits, but we learn more of his support of learning from Mussalman authors.

The best history of Mussalman India after Aurungzeb was written in Persian in Warren Hastings' time by Nawab Syed Ghulam Hosain Khan Taba-Tabai. He was a distinguished scholar and was held in high esteem by his English friends. He wrote also some poetry in the same language. The example, however, of Sauda gave a great impetus to the cultivation of Urdu, and thus, whilst historical and other literary works continued to be written

---

[1] The latter part of the 18th Century.

in Persian, Urdu became the vehicle for poetical thought; Sauda's Urdu is more Persian than Urdu—often in one couplet alone you can barely find more than two or three pure Urdu words. His contemporary Atesh was less given to this; Zauk, who followed them, did great service to the Urdu language. In the fifties before the dark days of the Mutiny, Delhi also witnessed a great revival. The unfortunate Bahadur Shah II, who died in exile in Rangoon, was a learned man, retiring in his habits, and devoted to the company of scholars and poets. One of the most famous among them was Asad-ullah Khan, surnamed Ghalib, who enjoyed the respect equally of Hindus, Muhammedans and Christians.

In recent times there lived at Lucknow some poets and litterateurs—men whom it was both a pleasure and a profit to know—Dabir, and the three gifted brothers whose poetical names were derived from a single root-word, Uns or friendship. The two eldest were famous as Anis and Monis. Two accomplished scholars who exercised great influence on Mussalman thought about this period were Moulana Moulvi Syed Karamat 'Ali al-Husaini-al-Jaunpuri and Shams ul-'Ulama Moulvi Kabir-ud-din Ahmed. The Syed was indeed a remarkable man. He left his home in Jaunpur at the age of nineteen to study in Persia. He spent there some eighteen years, studying at various centres of Mussalman learning, and meeting various scholars and distinguished men in the course of his travels. He was a friend of Arthur Conolly, the well-known traveller, whose life he saved twice in Turkestan. He enjoyed the friendship of Amir Dost Mohammad Khan of Kabul. Soon after his return to India, in 1838, he was made *Mutwalli* or Governor of the *Mohsin* Endowment at Hooghly,[1] which office he held up to his death in 1876. His Sunday breakfasts brought together some noted Muslim scholars, with one or two English friends. Among these, Mr. Montriou, a well-known barrister, was the most intimate. Whatever knowledge of Arabian philosophy I possess I owe to my revered friend Syed Karamat Ali. Moulvi Kabir-ud-din Ahmed is best remembered by his work with Col. Nassau Lees in editing the old Mussalman works on law and history.

In our own times Moulvi Zaka-ullah has written a comprehensive history of India comprising the Hindu, Mohammedan and British periods. It is a work of great merit and written in a critical historical vein. Happily we have still living amongst us men whose names are honoured among all Mussalmans as embodying the culture of Islam; Moulvi Altaf Hosain Khan Hali, Moulvi Mohammed Husain Azad, the author of the *Durbari-i-Akbari*, Moulana Shibli,[2] my highly respected friend Shams-ul-'Ulama Maulana 'Ali Mohammed Shad, whose great merits were not long ago recognised by the Indian Government, are known to many English officials.

The poems of Moulana Hali still help to rouse some enthusiasm for the learning and culture of his fore-fathers in the Mussalman youth whose blood has been chilled by Anglo-Mohammedan education.

No one to whom it has been vouchsafed to have a glimpse of the polished courtesy and dignified intercourse of the Mussalman gentry of the old school, who have either passed away or are fast passing away, will ever fail to

---

[1] A princely gift by a royal lady of Murshidabad, endowed for educational purposes.

[2] Alas ! both Moulana Hali and Moulana Shibli have died since this article was written.

regard it as a privilege. To me it is a memory to cherish. The sight of those dignified men, with their courtly manners, sitting together conversing in well-modulated tones which never rose to a noise, on history, poetry, literature, and Mussalman divinity, would be a revelation to many Western critics. Each man was attended by servants, including his own *hukka-bardar*; the reception of each guest as he arrived was dignified, in cases of intimate friends genial. As he took his seat, the *hukka-bardar* spread first the piece of brocade on which the hukka was placed, and bending on his knees handed to his master the gold and silver mouthpiece, with inimitable grace. The assembly, which often contained a sprinkling of young men of a serious turn of mind, with a long row of hukkas and their silver *chilams*, formed an agreeable sight.

Poetical assemblies were still held twenty years ago. But now debating clubs have taken their place. In the first half of the Nineteenth Century the *Mushairas* as they were called, were often attended by one or two English officials who, with their knowledge of Persian and Urdu, were able to follow and appreciate the poems that were recited. The name of Mr. Douglas, who was Collector of Bankipore in the 'Fifties, is remembered with respect.

The results of the change in Mussalman culture within the last twenty-five or thirty years remain to be seen. But I cannot help regretting the passing of the old order. Had it been possible to engraft the best part of European culture on the remains of Islamic culture, the awakening of Mussalman India would cause no misgiving. We can only watch anxiously the present development and trust that the hopes of helpers will be justified by the fruit borne by Anglo-Mohammedan culture.

NOTES

Munificent: very generous.

P. 134, l. 14. Notice the expression: *He cultivated the society of cultured scholars.* We speak of cultivating the society or friendship of people. *Cultured* is the word which many students should use when they write *educated*. Most people are educated to some extent; few are cultured, which means possessing not only knowledge but a character trained in the finer virtues, such as courtesy, care for the welfare of others, charm of manner, and moderation. All these words beginning with *cult-* are derived from a Latin word which means both *tilling the ground* and *worship*, which shows how words describing very ancient and simple actions of men can also convey the idea of his relation to his gods. The word *cult* in English means worship.

P. 134, l. 16. Babar severely put down any violence committed by his soldiers. *Soldiery* is a general term, *soldiers* a particular term.

Condign: fitting. **Administrative capacity:** power to govern.

Cope with: struggle against successfully.

Turbulent: rough and troublesome.

Firoz: Firoz Shah (1351-1370) who succeeded Mohamed Tughlaq as Mogul ruler.

Fiscal units: separate parts to be taxed. *Fiscal* is the adjective used to refer to public revenue.

Mediators: people who act between two other parties.

Assessment: fixing the rate of taxation.

Patrolled: watched by men on horseback who rode along it at appointed times. **Serais:** rest-houses.

Betook himself: went. **Shah Tahmasp:** ruler of Persia 1524-1576.

Influx: flowing in. **Moulding:** giving form to.

P. 137, l. 19. Bringing together into one the provinces which had broken up into separate governments.

Chaos: this word means extreme confusion. Originally *chaos* meant the state of the world before any order was developed from it. **Ordinances:** decrees.

Legacy: something a man leaves behind when he dies.

Unflinching: not drawing back from any duty.

Cornelian or **carnelian:** a dull red or reddish-white stone.

Pharmacist: a man who makes medicines.

Magnates: very wealthy people.

Fabulous: enormous. **Indulgent:** too kind.

Touching: touching or affecting our feelings.

Weaned: as a child is weaned from his mother's breast and taught to take other food.

Instigated it: persuaded some one to commit the murder.

Ignored: taken no notice of. **Faculty:** ability.

Enumeration: numbered account. **Cesses:** taxes.

Mutilation: cutting off parts of the body.
Acquisition: Acquiring, getting hold of.
Zenith: highest point. **Imbibed:** drunk in, learnt.
Galaxy: throng, crowd (*lit.* The Milky Way).
Litterateurs: a French word meaning men of letters. The French retain the double *t* while we have only one in *literature*.
Functionaries: officials. **Stringent:** strict.
Assigned: made over (to some one). **Plaintiff:** one who appeals.
Adjudication of: judgment on.
Tribunal: Court of justice or enquiry.
Ostentation: show, display. **Vicissitudes:** changes of fortune.
P. 148, l. 28. It shows how architecture can be made to express poetic feeling. **Setback to:** reversal of.
Ultra-orthodox: extremely strict in their religious views.
Capitation tax: a tax of so much a head.
Alienated: turned them away.
Estranged: made strangers or enemies of.
Impetus: stimulus, encouragement.
P. 150, l. 28. Urdu became the medium or mode of expression for poetry.

QUESTIONS

1. What are the characteristics of the Emperor Babar referred to at the beginning of this piece?
2. Summarize Babar's account of the people of Hindustan four hundred years ago.
3. What were the principal reforms of Sher Shah?
4. What does the author say about Persian influence in the time of Humayun?
5. What is told us about Akbar's administrative regulations?
6. Tell briefly the story of Asad Beg's experience with tobacco at Bijapur.
7. What was the Mina Bazar?
8. How does the author represent the character of Jahangir?
9. What does he say of Nur Jahan?
10. What were the chief regulations introduced by Jahangir?
11. How does the author characterize the Emperor Shah Jahan?
12. What did Rai Bhare Mal say about the condition of the country in Shah Jahan's reign?
13. What does the author tell us of the charity of Nur Jahan?
14. What view does the author take of Aurungzeb?
15. How does he refer to the courtesy and dignity of Mussalman gentry of the old school?

SUBJECTS FOR ESSAYS

1. On the Meaning of Culture.
2. Islamic Ideals.
3. Persian Influence on Indian Life.

XIV

THE GREATER INDIA TO BE

CONVOCATION ADDRESS[1]

BY SIR JAGADIS CHANDRA BOSE, F.R.S.

Sir J. C. Bose was born in 1859 at Dacca, graduated in Calcutta, and in 1884 took degrees at Cambridge and London. On his return to India he became professor of Physics in Calcutta and after some years, during which he published various articles on electricity, one of his papers was published by the Royal Society in London. He was one of the pioneers in wireless telegraphy, and it is claimed for him that in 1895 he was the first to show the possibilities in the transmission of waves of ether. In 1897 he lectured before the Royal Institution on Electrical Waves, and the honour was again shown him in 1901 and 1915.

The work by which he has become known all over the world is his study of the reactions of plants to various kinds of stimulation, on which subject he has lectured before the leading Universities of Europe, Asia and America, using for his experiments the most delicate instruments, made by Indian workmen.

In 1917 he opened his famous Research Institute in Calcutta, at which students from Europe and America also have studied. He is the inventor of an instrument called the Crescograph, which measures and magnifies the growth of plants even in a single second. He has startled the world by his analogy between animals and plants, in which he speaks of the perception and memory of plants, and for many years he has been illustrating this in his lectures illustrated by photographs of the movements of plants.

Sir J. C. Bose has also made his name as a writer and speaker, and many striking lectures on Indian ideals have been delivered by him at various universities.

The following memorable words were uttered by him at the conclusion of a lecture before the Royal Institution in London in 1902:

'It was when I came upon the mute witness of these self-made records and perceived in them one phase of pervading unity that bears within it all things,—the mote that quivers in ripples of light, the teeming life upon our earth, and the radiant suns that shine above us—it was then that I understood for the first time a

---

[1] Delivered at the University of Mysore.

little of that message proclaimed by my ancestors on the banks of the Ganges thirty centuries ago :—

"They who see but one in all the changing manifoldness of the universe, unto them belongs eternal truth, unto none else, unto none else."

MANY years ago I chose teaching not as a profession, but as the highest vocation. I could think of nothing higher than consecrating my life to the guidance of the young with their dreams and aspirations yet unfulfilled and in helping them in the attainment of manhood. I see before me young students going out into life's great adventure. What is to be the guiding principle that is to stand by you and inspire you even in days of despondency ? There never came a time so fateful as the present when a great demand is made on the strength and idealism of our youth in serving the highest interest of the country. I will not therefore appeal to your weakness but to your strength ; I would not care to set before you what is easy but use all compulsion for your choice of the most difficult. You are seekers after truth ; I will tell you of the discipline through which you must pass for the discovery of truth.

I have been, and am still, a student ; your struggles and difficulties have also been mine. In your hours of despondency it may perhaps help you to know that not even a glimmer of success ever came to remove the gloom except after years of persistent struggle. I hold the belief that it is not for man to complain of circumstances, but bravely to accept, to confront and dominate them. I know that what has been done before will be accomplished again and that the past was not to remain merely as a dream.

I spoke of my work itself being my teacher. The

illumination came to me only after years of unremitting pursuit of truth. It was this that enabled me, through rigid scientific methods, to establish the great generalisation of the Unity of Life and to realise fully all that it meant. I will tell you what I was able to decipher in the book of life itself, of conditions which exalt the highest manifestations of life.

The highest expression in the life of a nation must be its intellectual eminence and its power of enriching the world by advancing the frontiers of knowledge. When a nation has lost this power, when it merely receives and has nothing to give, then its healthy life is over and it sinks into a degenerate existence which is purely parasitic. The status of a great university cannot be secured by any artificial means, nor can any charter assure it. Its world status is only to be won by the intrinsic value of great contributions made by its scholars. To be organic and vital, our national university must stand primarily for self-expression and winning for India her true place among the federation of nations.

In regard to the spread of learning, geographical barriers have never in the past offered any obstacle to the intellectual communion among the different peoples of India. The vision of the past rises vividly before us, and we behold a great procession of immortals who still live and inspire us. We see Sankaracharya acclaimed everywhere during his march of intellectual conquest of all countries from the South to the extreme North. We see the scholars of Bengal with a few palm leaf manuscripts as their sole treasure, crossing the Himalayan barrier; inspired by love and service, they carry Indian lore to Tibet, to China, and to the further East. The great intellectual movements were never confined to any particular province, for the torch of learning was kept lighted for many centuries in her different universities. And it was the fame of a great teacher that drew scholars from even the most distant corners of India. The traditions of the past have not been lost, for even today leaders of thought from different provinces travel from one end of the country to the other, thus keeping alive the bond of unity and closest kinship. Those who have read history aright, realise the great assimilative power of Indian civilisation by which many races and peoples came to regard this great country as their home. And it is by their joint efforts that will be built the Greater India yet to be.

Nothing can be more vulgar or more untrue than the ignorant assertion that the world owes its progress of knowledge to any particular race. The whole world is interdependent and a constant stream of thought has throughout ages enriched the common heritage of mankind.

Can we remain satisfied only with the traditions of the past? Critics have told us time after time that whatever the past might have been, there is now no strength left for the renewal of our national life. They point out that while successful national efforts have been few and far between, the failures have been far too many. But failure is only transient, while success waits for us round the last corner. It is the obvious and the blatant that blind us to the essential. Few realise the great urge hidden to the eyes of men, that is moving the great mass of the people in their ceaseless efforts to realise some common aspiration. Where lies the secret of that power which makes certain efforts apparently doomed to failure rise renewed from beneath smouldering ashes? When we look deeper we shall find that as inevitable as is the sequence of cause and effect, so sure must be the sequence of failure and success.

Although science is neither of the East nor of the West but international in its universality, yet India by her habit of mind and inherited gifts handed down from generation to generation is specially fitted to make great contributions in advancing knowledge. The burning Indian imagination which can compel new order to come out of a mass of apparently contradictory facts, can also be held in check by the habit of concentration; it is this restraint which confers the power to hold the mind in pursuit of truth in infinite patience.

The real difficulty that thwarts the investigator of plant life arises from the fact that the life-action is taking place within the dark depths of the interior of the tree which our eyes cannot fathom. As the first step to discover the hidden mechanism of the tree, one has to become the tree and feel the pulse-beat of its throbbing life. Next, in order to reveal the intricate mechanism of its life, it is necessary to gain access to the smallest unit of life, the 'life atom' and succeed in recording its throbbing pulsation.

For this it was necessary to invent instruments of surpassing accuracy and sensitiveness. The invention of the microscope magnifying only a few thousand times initiated a new era in advance of biological science. The Magnetic Crescograph magnifying fifty million times is now revealing the wonders of the world, the plant itself being made to reveal the secrets of its inner life. Even in this path of self-restraint and verification, the inquirer is making for a region of surpassing wonder.

These wonders became revealed to me only after years

of struggle in overcoming difficulties which at first appeared as almost insurmountable. It was the Indian habit of concentration that led ultimately to the overcoming of all difficulties. It is no easy life that lies before an investigator. He has to steel his body and mind to the utmost, and prepare for a life of unending struggle. Even after all this there is no assurance whatever of success to reward him for his ceaseless toil. He has to cast his life as an offering, regarding gain and loss, success and failure, as one. But the lure that draws heroic souls is not success that can be easily achieved, but defeat and tribulation in the pursuit of the unattainable.

Increasing unemployment and severe economic distress are the cause of unrest here as in other parts of the world; only on account of its magnitude the problem is far more acute here. It is hunger that drives people to desperation and to the destruction of all that has been built up for ordered progress. It is tragic that our own country with its great potential wealth and possibilities of industrial development should be in this plight. All efforts have been long paralysed by assertions, as ignorant as they are unfounded, that this country is incapable of producing great discoverers and inventors. These assertions have now been completely disproved by the fact that the extraordinarily sensitive instruments by which the new discoveries have been rendered possible have been all constructed by Indian mechanicians.

In other parts of the world, it is the best intellect of the country and the leading men of business—who are called to devise means for increasing the wealth of the country. In my travels I found little or no distress in small countries such as Norway and Denmark, countries which are in no sense rich in natural wealth. Nevertheless they have their system of universal education and the most up to date universities. Could we not take to heart the lesson thus taught? There are now a very large number of young men who could be specially trained in efficiently conducted institutes, the standard of which should bear comparison with any in the world. It should be also our aim not to be so entirely dependent on foreign countries for our higher education and for our needs. For carrying out such a programme, a far-sighted State policy is urgently required.

When man beheld spread before him the earth, the sea and the air, he went forth in his great adventures. He rode the tumultuous sea and circled the globe. The challenge of the sky he accepted and by his daring spirit conquered it and established an unobstructed highway. Man is a creative being and these miracles attest to his godlike and indomitable spirit. But the weakling, who has forgotten the divinity that is in him, leads an ignoble life of passivity. He alone who has striven and won can enrich the world by giving away the fruits of his victorious experience.

A strange weakness and passivity has entered into the life of the people, and unless the evil is remedied, the end is inevitable. Nature shows no mercy to the feeble and the decadent. The vicious circle lies in this: the lazy is content with earning what is barely sufficient to maintain life itself; the evil increases at a compound rate, reducing further the capacity for work, and also the power of resistance to ills that beset life, ending in the lowering of the scale of human life, starvation and death. In other countries even under stress of great national disaster, human efficiency has remained unimpaired, due to the joint efforts of the people and the State in building up national prosperity.

There is a special need for an enlightened policy in regard to the shaping of the post-graduate career of the most distinguished students of an Indian university. Many of my old students showed special aptitude in science; but as there was no scientific career open to them, they were compelled against their natural inclination to choose the uncertain profession of law.

In contrast to this, I have had the opportunity of becoming acquainted with the solicitude with which the Government of Japan follows the career of her promising students, whom they regard as the greatest asset for the advancement of their country. I found them personally known at headquarters, and arrangements made through Japanese Consuls in Europe and America, so that in the course of two years they go through a very arduous training under the most distinguished specialists to make them efficient in their subjects. They do not find themselves stranded on their return, for arrangements have already been made by their Government, so that their intellect and training find the fullest scope in the service of the State.

This leads me to the ideal of a model State which finds practical expression in the establishment of the national university and in many enterprises for the welfare of the people. The university and the industrial enterprises cannot be dissociated from each other but must be regarded as complementary activities for the common good of the State.

Teaching and research are indissolubly connected with each other. The spirit of research cannot be imparted by mere lectures on antiquated theories which are often entirely baseless and which effectively block all further progress. Nothing can be so destructive of originality as blind acceptance of authoritative statements. The true function of a great teacher is to train his disciples to discover things themselves. Such a teacher cannot be easily found and it will be the duty of the university to discover him and give him every facility for his work. Let there be no creation of a learned caste whose attention is mainly taken up in securing special privileges. It is only from a burning candle that others should be lighted. The pupils by working under such a teacher will learn the value of persistence and of the infinite care to be taken at every step; they will catch from him glimpses of inspiration by which he succeeds in wresting from Nature her most jealously guarded secrets. They will become a part of his being and will hand down a passionate love of truth through fleeting generations. That spirit can never die; we shall pass away, and even kingdoms may disappear. Truth alone will survive, for it is eternal.

What is to be my message to young students with whom I am brought in touch today? Could I wish for you anything less than that you should attain the highest manhood or womanhood? May you realise the great privilege of being born at a time when your country needed you most! The civilisation we have inherited has lasted through many milleniums; you will certainly not allow it to be destroyed through weakness or passivity. You will answer to this call that has been echoing through ages, the call which compels men and women to choose a life of unending struggle, for the alleviation of human suffering. It was action and not weak passivity that was glorified in heroic India of the past and the greatest illumination came even in the field of battle.

There can be no happiness for any of us, unless it has been won for all. In this I would urge on you the doctrine of strength and of undying hope. Realise that there is something in the Indian culture which is possessed of extraordinary latent strength by which it has resisted the ravages of time and destructive changes that have swept over the earth. And indeed a capacity to endure through infinite transformations must be innate in that mighty civilisation which has seen the intellectual culture of the Nile Valley, of Assyria and of Babylonia, wax, wane and disappear, and which today gazes on the future with the same invincible faith with which it met the past.

NOTES

Vocation: life-work, calling.
Glimmer: faint light.
To confront and dominate: to face and master.
Unremitting: never given up.
Generalization of: general declaration about.
Decipher: make out, understand.
Eminence: height, distinction.
P. 158, l. 10. Moving forward the limits of knowledge.
Degenerate: sunk from a higher condition, decaying.
Parasitic: feeding or living on others.
Barriers: something that prevents advance (in this case seas and mountains).
Acclaimed: praised.
Assimilative power: power to take in things and make them suitable for one's own use.
Heritage: inheritance.
Failure is only for a time: we shall succeed after making the last effort necessary.
Blatant: vulgarly noisy.
P. 160, ll. 1-3. When we look deeper we shall find that just as cause is unavoidably followed by effect, so success is sure to follow failure.
Thwarts: disappoints, hinders.

Throbbing pulsation: beating pulse.
Crescograph: an instrument invented by Prof. Bose which magnifies the process of growth.
Lure: attraction.
Tribulation: suffering.
Magnitude: great size.
Indomitable: untamable, unconquerable.
Unimpaired: undamaged.
Aptitude: fitness.
Stranded: like a ship on shore, unable to move, without employment.
Antiquated: out-of-date.
Wresting: dragging by force.
Millenium: a thousand years.
Passivity: the opposite of activity.
Alleviation: relief.
Invincible: unconquerable.

QUESTIONS

1. What does Sir Jagadis say about our choice of the more difficult way?
2. What does he regard as necessary to enhance the status of a University?
3. What is his great hope for the building of the Greater India?
4. What does he say in reply to critics of natural success?
5. How did he come to his unique knowledge of plant life?
6. What is the Crescograph?
7. What has been the author's experience of the life of an investigator?
8. What are the lessons India may learn from Norway and Denmark?
9. What criticism does the author make of Indian passivity?
10. How are gifted students encouraged in Japan?
11. What message has Sir Jagadis for teachers and students?

SUBJECTS FOR ESSAYS

1. The Task Facing India.
2. Overcoming Difficulties.
3. Man's Advance in Knowledge.
4. Education in a Model State.

I

A SERMON ON GOD

By Mahatma Gandhi

Because of the high place which our friend Mr. Gandhi holds in every Indian heart, it would be presumptuous of me to say much here, except to express my gratitude to him for his permission to include these three beautiful pieces in this little book.

There has recently been published what we call an Omnibus book of the writings and speeches of Mr. Gandhi, nearly eleven hundred pages of earnest, thoughtful English. This book is for me typical of the effort India has made to rise above herself by undergoing the long and hard discipline of higher self-expression in a foreign language, a language on the difficulty of which Mr. Gandhi has himself written. The need for this discipline, however regrettable it may be considered by those who resent it, has certainly had the magnificent result of far more Indians being able to impress their personalities on the English-speaking world than the people of any other foreign country have succeeded in doing. It has added greatly to the spiritual wealth of the world. Moreover, Mr. Gandhi's remarkable facility in writing crystal-clear argumentative English, will bring history into considerable debt to him.

Mahatma Gandhi, by virtue of his long struggle, has become a desirable factor in the education of the world to-day: his example is as necessary to the people of Italy or Turkey as that of their own great leaders. Few have been so worthy as he to stand in the company of those who have so strenuously debated on the future of India.

(When the Columbia Gramophone Company requested Mahatma Gandhi to make a record for them, he pleaded inability to speak on politics, and added that, at the age of 60, he could make only his first and last record, which should, if wanted, make his voice heard for all time. Confessing his anxiety to speak on spiritual matters, which are of deep and everlasting interest as against purely political matters, which are only of transient interest, Mahatma Gandhi spoke as follows.)

There is an indefinable mysterious Power that pervades everything. I feel it though I do not see it.

It is this unseen power which makes itself felt and that defies all proof because it is so unlike all that I perceive through my senses. It transcends the senses because it is possible to reason out the existence of God only to a limited extent.

Even in ordinary affairs we know that people do not know Who rules or why or how He rules, but that they know that there is a Power that certainly rules.

In my tour, some years ago, of Mysore, I met many poor villagers and I found, upon inquiry, that they did not know who ruled Mysore. They simply said some God ruled it. If the knowledge of these people was so limited about their ruler, I, who am an infinitely lesser being in respect to God than they to their ruler, need not be surprised if I do not realise the presence of God, the King of Kings. Nevertheless, I do feel, as the poor villagers felt about Mysore, that there is orderliness in the universe, there is an unalterable law governing everything and every being that exists or lives.

It is not a blind law, for no blind law can govern the conduct of living beings, and, thanks to the marvellous researches of Sir J. C. Bose, it can now be proved that even matter is life. That law, then, which governs all life is God.

The law and the Law-giver are one. I may not deny the law or the Law-giver, because I know so little about it or Him. Just as my denial or ignorance of the existence of an earthly power will avail me nothing, even so my denial of God and His law will not liberate me from its operation, whereas a humble and mute acceptance of Divine Authority makes life's journey easier even as the acceptance of earthly rule makes life under it easier. I do perceive that whilst everything around me is ever-changing and ever-dying, there is, underlying all that change, a living Power that is changeless, that holds all together, that creates, dissolves and recreates. That informing Power of Spirit is God. And since nothing else that I see merely through the senses can or will persist, He alone is.

And is this Power benevolent or malevolent? I see it as purely benevolent, for I can see that, in the midst of death, life persists; in the midst of untruth, truth persists; in the midst of darkness, light persists. Hence I gather that God is life, truth and light. He is love, He is the Supreme Good.

But He is no God who merely satisfies the intellect, if He ever does. God, to be God, must rule the heart and transform it. He must express Himself in every smallest act of His votary. This can be done only through a definite realisation more real than the five senses can ever produce. Sense perceptions can be and often are false and deceptive, however real they may appear to us. Where there is realisation outside the senses, it is infallible. It is proved not by extraneous evidence but in the transformed conduct and character of those who have felt the real presence of God within.

Such testimony is to be found in the experiences of an unbroken line of prophets and sages in all countries and climes. To reject this evidence is to deny oneself. This realisation is preceded by immovable faith. He who would in his own person test the fact of God's presence can do so by living faith, and since faith itself cannot be proved by extraneous evidence the safest course is to believe in the moral government of the world, and therefore, in the supremacy of the moral law—the law of truth and love.

Exercise of faith will be the safest, where there is a clear determination summarily to reject all that is contrary to truth and love.

I confess that I have no argument to convince through reason. Faith transcends reason. All I can advise is not to attempt the impossible.

I cannot account for the existence of evil by any rational method. To want to do so is to want to be co-equal with God. I am, therefore, humble enough to recognise evil as such and I call God long-suffering and patient precisely because He permits evil in the world. I know that He has no evil in Himself and yet if there be evil He is the author of it and yet untouched by it.

I know, too, that I shall never know God if I do not wrestle with and against evil even at the cost of life itself. I am fortified in this belief by my own humble and limited experience. The purer I try to become, the nearer to God I feel myself to be. How much more should I be near to Him when my faith is not a mere apology as it is today, but has become as immovable as the Himalayas and as white as the snows on their peaks!

II

PRAYER

By Mahatma Gandhi

Prayer has saved my life. Without it, I should have been a lunatic long ago. I have had my share of the bitterest public and private experiences. They threw me into temporary despair. If I was able to get rid of that despair, it was because of prayer. Prayer has not been a part of my life as truth has been. Prayer came out of sheer necessity. I found myself in a plight where I could not possibly be happy without prayer. The more my faith in God increased, the more irresistible became the yearning for prayer. Life seemed to be dull and vacant without it.

I had attended the Christian religious services in South Africa, but they failed to grip me. My Christian friends supplicated God, but I could not do so. I failed grievously. I started with a disbelief in God and prayer. And until at a late stage in life I did not feel anything like a void in life. At that state, I felt that as food was indispensable to the body, so was prayer indispensable for the soul. In fact, food for the body is not so necessary as prayer for the soul. For starvation is often necessary in order to keep the body in health, but there is no such thing as prayer-starvation. You cannot possibly have a surfeit of prayer.

Three of the greatest teachers of the world, Buddha, Jesus, and Mohammed, have left unimpeachable testimony that they found illumination through prayer and could not possibly live without it. Millions of Christians, Hindus and Mussalmans find their only solace in life in prayer. Either you vote them down as liars, or as self-deluded people. I will say that this 'lying' has a charm for me, a truth-seeker, if it is 'lying' that has given me that mainstay or staff to life, without which I could not dare to live for a moment. In spite of despair staring me in the face on the political horizon, I have never lost my peace. In fact, I have found people who envy my peace. That peace comes from prayer.

I am not a man of learning, but I humbly claim to be a man of prayer. I am indifferent as to the form. Every one is a law unto himself in that respect. But there are some well-marked roads, and it is safe to walk along the beaten tracks trodden by the ancient teachers.

It is beyond my power to induce in you a belief in God. There are certain things which are self-proved and certain things which are not proved at all. The existence of God is like a geometrical axiom. It may be beyond our heart-grasp. I shall not talk of an intellectual grasp. Intellectual attempts are more or less fallacious, as a rational explanation cannot give you the faith in a living God. For it is a thing beyond the grasp of reason. It transcends reason.

There are various phenomena from which you can reason out the existence of God, but I shall not insult your intelligence by offering you a rational explanation of that type. I would have you brush aside all rational explanations and begin with a simple child-like faith in God. If I exist, God exists. With me it is a necessity of my being, as it is with millions. They may not be able to talk about it, but from their life you can see that it is part of their very souls.

III

VOLUNTARY POVERTY

By Mahatma Gandhi

When I found myself drawn into the political whirl, I asked myself what was necessary for me in order to remain absolutely untouched by immorality, by untruth, by what is known as political gain . . . . I do not propose to take you through all the details of that act or performance, interesting and, to me, sacred though they are—but I can only tell you that it was a difficult struggle in the beginning and it was a wrestle with my wife and—as I can vividly recall—with my children also. Be that as it may, I came definitely to the conclusion that, if I had to serve the people in whose midst my life was cast and of whose difficulties I was witness from day to day, I must discard all wealth, all possession.

I cannot tell you with truth that, when this belief came to me, I discarded everything immediately. I must confess to you that progress at first was slow. And now, as I recall those days of struggle I remember that it was also painful in the beginning. But, as days went by, I saw that I had to throw overboard many other things which I used to consider as mine, and a time came when it became a matter of positive joy to give up those things. And one after another then the things slipped away from me. And, as I am describing my experiences, I can say a great burden fell off my shoulders, and I felt that I could now walk with ease and do my work also in the service of my fellowmen with great comfort and still greater joy. The possession of anything then became a troublesome thing and a burden.

Exploring the cause of that joy, I found that, if I kept anything as my own, I had to defend it against the whole world. I found also that there were many people who did not have the thing, although they wanted it; and I would have to seek police assistance also if hungry famine-stricken people, finding me in a lonely place, wanted not merely to divide the thing with me but to dispossess me. And I said to myself: If they want it and would take it, they do so not from any malicious motive, but they would do it because theirs was a greater need than mine.

And then I said to myself: Possession seems to me to be a crime: I can only possess certain things when I know that others, who also want to possess similar things, are able to do so. But we know—every one of us can speak from experience—that such a thing is an impossibility. Therefore, the only thing that can be possessed by all is non-possession, not to have anything whatsoever. In other words, a willing surrender.

You might then well say to me: But you are keeping many things on your body even as you are speaking about voluntary poverty and not possessing anything whatsoever! And your taunt would be right, if you only a little understood the meaning of the thing that I am speaking about just now. It is really the spirit behind. Whilst you have the body, you will have to have something to clothe the body with also. But then you will take for the body not all that you can get, but the least possible, the least with which you can do. You will take for your house not many mansions, but the least cover that you can do with. And similarly with reference to your food and so on.

Now you see that there is here a daily conflict between what you and we understand today as civilization and the state which I am picturing to you as a state of bliss and a desirable state. On the other hand, the basis of culture for civilization is understood to be the multiplication of all your wants. If you have one room, you will desire to have two rooms, three rooms, the more the merrier. And similarly, you will want to have as much furniture as you can put in your house, and so on, endlessly. And the more you possess, the better culture you represent, or some such thing. I am putting it, perhaps, not as nicely as those who praise that civilization would put it, but I am putting it to you in the manner I understand it.

And, on the other hand, you find the less you possess, the less you want, the better you are. And better for what? Not for enjoyment of this life, but for enjoyment of personal service to your fellow-beings; service to which you dedicate yourselves, body, soul and mind .... even the body is not yours. It has been given to you as a temporary possession, and it can also be taken from you by Him who has given it to you.

Therefore, having that absolute conviction in me, such must be my constant desire, that this body also may be surrendered at the will of God, and while it is at my disposal, must be used not for dissipation, not for self-indulgence, not for pleasure, but merely for service the whole of my waking hours. And if this is true with reference to the body, how much more with reference to clothing and other things that we use?

And those who have actually followed out this view of voluntary poverty to the fullest extent possible (to reach absolute perfection is an impossibility, but the fullest possible extent for a human being), those who have reached the ideal of that state, they testify that when you dispossess yourself of everything you have, you really possess all the treasures of the world. In other words, you really get all that is in reality necessary for you, in everything. If food is necessary, food will come to you.

Many of you are men and women of prayer, and I have heard from very many Christian people that they got their food in answer to prayer, that they get everything in answer to prayer. I believe it. But I want you to come with me a step further and believe with me that those who voluntarily give up everything on earth, including the body—that is to say, have readiness to give up everything (and they must examine themselves critically, sternly, and always give judgment against themselves)—those who will follow this out will really find that they are never in want.

Want must not, again, be taken literally. God is the hardest task-master I have known on this earth, and He tries you through and through. And when you find that your faith is failing or your body is failing you, and you are sinking, He comes to your assistance somehow or other and proves to you that you must not lose your faith and that He is always at your beck and call, but on His terms, not on your terms. So I have found. I cannot really recall a single instance when, at the eleventh hour, He has forsaken me.

NOTES

I

Pervades: moves through.
Transcends: goes beyond.
P. 168, l. 29. Will not set me free from obedience of His law.
Informing: inspiring.
Benevolent or malevolent: these are Latin participles meaning *wishing well or wishing evil,* good or bad.
Infallible: incapable of being wrong.
Extraneous: outside.

II

Lunatic: a mad person.
Supplicated: begged.
Void: an emptiness.
Surfeit: too much.
Unimpeachable:, that cannot be found fault with.

Self-deluded: deceived by themselves.
Axiom: a self-evident truth.
Fallacious: false, deceptive.

III

Malicious: evil.
P. 174, l. 10. Giving oneself up willingly.
Taunt: reproach.
Dissipation: frivolous or wasteful amusement.

QUESTIONS

1. What analogy did Mr. Gandhi use with reference to his relation to God?
2. How does Mr. Gandhi think of God?
3. What are his convictions regarding Faith?
4. And how does he feel he can come to have knowledge of God?
5. What value has Mr. Gandhi learnt to set on prayer?
6. What does he say about the existence of God?
7. What was Mr. Gandhi's experience in giving up the possession of things?
8. What is the principle on which he practises renunciation?
9. What is his experience as the result of embracing poverty?

SUBJECTS FOR ESSAYS

1. Our Relation to God.
2. My Experience of Prayer.
3. The Nature of Prayer.
4. Whether Possession is an Evil or a Sacred Trust.
5. Indian Poverty.